RHYTHMS, RITES AND RITUALS
My Life in Japan in Two-step and Waltz-time

Derek and Dorothy at her cousin Pat Hiller Chadwick's house, London, after her investiture of the MBE, 2010, at Buckingham Palace

RHYTHMS, RITES AND RITUALS

My Life in Japan in
Two-step and Waltz-time

by

Dorothy Britton

RENAISSANCE BOOKS

RHYTHMS, RITES AND RITUALS
MY LIFE IN TWO-STEP AND WALTZ-TIME

By Dorothy Britton

First published 2015 by
RENAISSANCE BOOKS
PO Box 219
Folkestone
Kent CT20 2WP

www.renaissancebooks.co.uk

Renaissance Books is an imprint of Global Books Ltd

ISBN 978-1-898823-12-4

SPECIAL THANKS

The Publishers wish to express their grateful
thanks to the Great Britain-Sasakawa Foundation
and The Tokyo Club for their generous
contribution towards the making of this book.

British Library Cataloguing in Publication Data
A catalogue record for this book is available from the British
Library

Typeset in Bembo 13 on 15 by Dataworks.
Printed and bound in England by CPI Antony Rowe

To my Parents
And three wonderful men in my life:
'Boy', Ikuma and 'Ted'.
And, of course, darling Derek,
my delightful 'walking doll'

Contents

✦

Preface

✦

MY LIFE HAS been so full of remarkable friendships that this book could have gone on and on. I wish I could have told about all of them. They usually had fascinating beginnings, too. The Australian actress Geraldine Ward was sitting opposite us on a train from Hastings to London, and was so mystified by Derek, in his father's RAF blazer, who seemed unable to speak. She came to the conclusion he must have suffered a plane crash in the war and she started a sympathetic conversation. We became friends, and she used to visit us in Japan on her way to Australia, and we always got together when in London. Then there was the phone call from a Japanese secretary at the US Naval Base in Yokosuka, who knew I was the widow of an RAF air marshal, and thought I might be interested to know that a lady Captain had just arrived with a retired British air force commander husband. When I rang him, he said yes, he was a commander – but in the Royal Navy! 'You sound English,' he said. 'Let's meet.' And Ted and Derek and I became very close friends of the interesting Balink-Whites, whom we visited in their home in Florida as well as in New Zealand where she was once posted – the only country which agreed to take a female naval attaché!

And there was a remarkable coincidence. A group of high school teachers from the USA came to my house to hear about my translating Japanese literature. When I had finished talking, and we were having refreshments, one of the women casually mentioned that her great aunt had been killed in the Great Earthquake in Yokohama. My spine tingled, and I asked if her name was Edith Lacy. Next day I took her to see the grave with our aunts' names upon it. And then there was Edna Read, whom Paul Norbury, my wonderful publisher, asked me to meet to persuade her to write her own extraordinary Anglo-Japanese story.

And what would Derek and I have done without the Hoiseths? Our grocer all of a sudden introduced our neighbour Rodney who was in need of a blurb for his splendid book for learning English. We became friends, and eventually since they were unencumbered with children, he and his lovely wife Junko agreed to share my house with Derek and me after Ted passed away. I take Derek with me almost everywhere, but occasionally it is not possible, and since I do not like to leave him at home alone, it is marvellous to be able to ask the Hoiseths to keep an eye on him. Like my husband Boy, Junko has a 'green thumb' when it comes to plants and flowers, so thanks to her our tiny garden always looks lovely. And dear Rodney knows all about computers! We get along so well and feel like family. What a wonderful coincidence that Rodney needed that blurb! My whole life has been an example of how intertwined our karma is, and how one thing leads to another.

JAPANESE NAMES

Throughout this memoir I have presented Japanese names according to Western styling, that is, with the given name first followed by the family name. Also, for the sake of simplicity, I have avoided using the macron to mark the long vowel in Japanese words comprising an 'o' or 'u'. I hope my scholarly friends will not be too critical of this decision!

DB

List of Plates

✦

CHAPTER 1

Rhythms Are What Divide Us

✦

I WAS A bonny baby, as most small children are, and my nanny called me a *bep-pin,* a colloquial term meaning 'a beauty', 'a knock-out'. There was, of course, the added glamour of my being a foreign baby. But my nanny soon shortened that and added *chan,* the affectionate suffix, giving me the nickname 'O-bet-chan'. All my old Japanese friends still call me that – even including one princess! And as with most Japanese nicknames, the origin is not clear.

From the moment she first laid eyes on me in Yokohama, Suzu Numano, my mother's first Japanese friend, from San Francisco days, called me 'The Japanese child with the Western skin'. For born in Japan, I have lived most of my life in two rhythms: the 'one-two, one-two' of Japanese, and English, which is mostly in waltz time. From the time I was a child I was fascinated by the differences in rhythm, and it seemed to me to affect not only the language but everyday life as well. I became very conscious of the fact that Japanese people seemed to move and walk in 2/4 time, while foreigners waltzed about. Footwear may have had something to do with it, for in those days the air was redolent with the *kak-ko kak-ko* sound of *geta*, while the heel-ball-toe with a shoe was a 1,2,3. And when they talked, Japanese people made little nods in 2/4 time, while Westerners' heads stayed still.

By the age of three, I had learned to read and my favourite book was *Through the Looking glass* by *Alice in Wonderland* author Lewis Carroll. In it Alice pokes the mirror that sits above the mantelpiece and enters the room that she sees in the mirror. It is the same room, but slightly different – a reflected version of it. Everything is the other way around. And I discovered I could enter a slightly different *world* in another way – just by speaking Japanese! That was *my* magic looking glass!

And, of course, I spoke it with the right rhythm, like the Japanese spoke it, simply having copied my Japanese nanny; so I seemed to really enter Japan and become Japanese. I thought it was tremendous fun going backwards and forwards between Japan and my parents' worlds, just as Alice went backwards and forwards through the looking glass! And I still do. And just as Alice's room in the mirror remained the same, people from every country and race have always seemed the same to me, with the only difference being the rhythm of their languages. I had made a wonderful discovery: that it is only rhythms that divide us!

I used to love going with my nanny to the Japanese festival at the local shrine, where the festival music, called *hayashi*, was in vigorously lilting 2/4 time. ('Shrine' is the customary English translation of *jinja*, the Shinto sanctum, whereas in Japan our word 'temple' is only used for *o-tera*, the Buddhist sanctuary.) Especially out in the countryside, one of the most important occasions in Japan's year is the annual village festival. These *o-matsuri* are Shinto festivals of supplication and thanksgiving for bumper crops and catches. They last for several days and are a time of general merrymaking. Fancy stalls are set up in the shrine compound, and stages are erected where plays are performed, as well as bouts of exhibition Sumo. I used to love the comic duo *hyot-toko* and *o-kamé,* and I still have a smiling *okamé* mask hanging in my study to keep me cheered up!

During the festival, the deity of the shrine is taken for a jolly outing in a small portable shrine carried this way and that on the shoulders of the young men of the village. Their task is made merrier all along the way by sips of *saké,* and by the end of the procession the god is usually rollicking all over the place, and giving its bearers a very hard time! Shrines everywhere, not only those in the villages, but every shrine in Japan

3

has its own festival. In towns and cities the god in his portable shrine has to cope with heavy traffic and is usually escorted by one or more policemen to keep back the cars. As they warm to the task, the lads that shoulder the mini-shrine set up a lusty antiphonal chorus shouting *wasshoi-wasshoi, wasshoi-wasshoi* (literally 'heave ho', but it is also a 'unifying' chant) half of them shouting the first *wasshoi* while the others reply with the second, creating a very infectious 1/2, 1/2 rhythm.

I used to have fun with my young Japanese friends by taking each others' names and singing them in festival music rhythm, for instance Takeko would go '*take-take kok-ko, take kok-ko*' and then I would go '*doro-doro thith-thee, doro-thith-thee*'. The Japanese pronunciation of my surname Britton was even better, sounding like a drum: *buri-buri ton-ton, buri-ton-ton!* When I was playing with my Japanese friends it was all in 2/4 rhythm, and I virtually 'became' Japanese!

And I found one did not have to be born in another country to learn how to 'sound' just like the people of that country. When I was seven or eight, my mother arranged for me to have French lessons from a French nun in Yokohama. All that nice nun did in my first lesson was to teach me to sing one single song sounding just like a French child. So I found that by sounding French I could 'enter' France now too. I soon became friends with three French girls, the daughters of the French consul. When we met again many years later in France, they told me how lots of American and British children in Yokohama were taking French lessons, but that I was the only one it was fun to play with, because I was the only one who really 'sounded' French. I am absolutely certain it is that first step that is so important in learning a foreign language: getting the sound and rhythm right. Spending time going over and over and over first words, then sentences, until you get it sounding just right. It takes time, but it is well worth it!

I once tried 'sounding' Dutch, too. I was a waitress in a club for sailors during the war in Bermuda, when some men from a Free Dutch Navy ship came in. I learned a few Dutch phrases such as 'Which would you like, tea or coffee?' getting the pronunciation as perfect as I could, which prompted them to begin conversations, but of course I was soon out of my depth, and would then have to disappear!

It does not matter how good your grammar is if it does not 'sound' like the language. I remember once going with my mother to a church in Geneva for the service in English. But the vicar's sermon did not sound like English at all and we could not understand a word. And though it sounded French, it was not French!

It happened so often in Tokyo at Embassy receptions, that a professor of English from some university would greet my mother in English, and she would turn to me and ask me to interpret, which was always so embarrassing. He was usually a highly respected professor, and his grammar was perfect, but it just did not SOUND like English!

When I speak Japanese, it sounds like Japanese, so people often think I *am* Japanese. I was having dinner in London once at the house of a Japanese friend from the Japanese Embassy. All the other guests were Japanese, and one of them said, 'Isn't it nice, all of us being Japanese, and no Brits present.' I was thrilled.

And then there was the time I asked a taxi driver to stop at the NHK building while I left my Irish harp there for a later performance. When I came out, he would not let me get in and instead pointed to the car in front. But the driver in front pointed to the taxi behind. So I went back. 'Did your passenger have a harp?' I asked him. He replied, 'Yes, but she was not a foreigner. She was Japanese.'

So few people seem to realize that the most important first step in learning a foreign language is getting the rhythm and sound right! For the sound, of course, is paramount too. That is why using *katakana*[1] when learning English is a no-no with its paucity of sounds. We apparently visualize the sounds we utter. So it is difficult to utter sounds that are not in one's written language. A Japanese sound that is very difficult for Western speakers is the syllable written in Roman letters with a consonant followed by a 'y': *kyo* as in *senkyo* (election) and *myo* as in *myonichi* (tomorrow). English people invariably pronounce two-syllable 'Kyoto' in three syllables, as Ki-o-to or even 'Kai-o-to', and usually two-syllable *byo-in* (hospital) as *bi-o-in* (beauty parlour)!

---

[1] A phonetic 'shorthand' syllabary containing fifty-six symbols used mainly now for writing foreign names and loan words. The more cursive *hiragana* is used for Japanese words.

A Chinese lady once told me that the reason the Chinese were so good at learning languages was because they have so many different sounds in Chinese - even more different sounds than we have in English! I knew a Japanese teacher of English who used to say that English in *kana* was pathetic English, and it certainly is pathetic the way Japanese *kana* can change so many English words into some that may even be embarrassing, for instance 'erection' for 'election'! I strongly believe that the Ministry of Education,[2] should introduce more kana. The vowel ウ (u) with diacritical dots ヴ for 'vu' is already used unofficially, for English words like 'dove' (*da-vu*). But those marks could be used on all five vowels to make a whole 'v' column: va-vi-vu-ve-vo. And then, an 'l' column, la-li-lu-le-lo, could be made by adding dots to ra-ri-ru-re-ro. And the sa-shi-su-se-so column could use the tiny diacritical circles to make tha-thi-thu-the-tho! That is only a start, of course, since there are many gaps in the other columns.

But at least, surely, a la-li-lu-le-lo column would be very, very useful?

And now, let me tell you how it happened that I was born in Japan.

---

[2] Now known as the Ministry of Education, Culture, Sport, Science and Technology (MEXT) – in Japanese 'Mombu-kagakushu'.

CHAPTER 2

My Mother

✦

MY MOTHER, ALICE Hiller, was born in San Francisco, granddaughter of a former Prussian count. Like Prince Chichibu in Japan, Count Johann Friedrich von Hill-erscheidt was greatly distressed by the hard lives of the poor German people, and at the time of the 1840 and 1841 uprisings known as the 'bread riots' he tried to help them. This got Friedrich into trouble with the Prussian authorities. They banished the young nobleman and confiscated his property, which led to his emigrating to the United States of America with his family.

Johann Friedrich had studied medicine and surgery at Heidelberg University, and while serving as a surgeon to Kaiser Wilhelm in the elite Black Hussars during the Franco-Prussian Wars, he married Hortense Parisot, the daughter of the mayor of a town in Alsace Lorraine. The vineyard-owning Parisots were a noble and ancient Provençal family descended from the Counts of Toulouse.

Johann Friedrich became a US citizen in 1849, and as Dr John Frederick Hiller MD he ministered with great popularity to the gold diggers of early Nevada. His son, Dr J. Frederick Hiller Jr followed in his footsteps as a general practitioner in San Francisco, where his daughter Alice, my mother, was born. She was a motley European mixture of German, French, Dutch and Scottish, and, when she travelled abroad, she used to complain that there was never enough space on the required form in the place for 'ethnic background', and she used to wonder how long it would be before one could just put 'American'! She longed to know the details of her grandfather's Prussian experience, but he refused to speak of the people who had angered him so much. 'I'm American now,' he would say in heavily accented English.

After years of gazing out across San Francisco Bay quoting to herself from Tennyson's *Ulysses:* 'My purpose holds to sail beyond the sunset,' Alice, when still quite young, had briefly visited the Philippines, and also spent a year in China with her best friend Alice Baker Richards, whose husband was working there. To join them in Chungking, she had to make a long but fascinating trip up the then magnificent Yang Tse River, which she describes in an article she wrote for the May 1918 issue of *The Record*, the San Francisco YWCA's magazine, one of whose editors she was. It is entitled 'Fifteen hundred miles on the Yangtse Kiang.' In it she writes:

Much of the charm of China lies in the mediaeval walls which enclose so many of the cities, the gates of which are closed at sunset and opened at sunrise, with the noisy beating of tom-toms and gongs.

And she goes on to say:

In the interior of China, things are now exactly as they must have been in the time of Marco Polo, and everything seems age-old. As we neared Chunking in the province of Szechuan, we were almost in sight of the Tibetan Hills, as they call the Himalayas. In Chungking one goes about in chairs carried by four bearers. There are no streets or roads, only paths, and miles of crowded stone steps. It is bewildering to have the coolies run up a steep flight of steps, with you almost falling out of the chair backwards on your head. The flowers of Szechuan are lovely, and golden pheasants lend color to the landscape.

Alice's interest in the Far East had already begun with her friendship with Suzu Numano, the wife of Yasutaro, the extremely handsome, Spanish-looking Consul-General of Japan. They gave wonderful parties, at which Suzu sang fascinating old traditional Japanese songs, accompanying herself on the *koto*, the long horizontal plucked instrument with a harp-like tone whose place in the Japanese upper-class home is like that of the parlour piano in the West. It was at one of the Numanos' parties that Alice met Opal, a talented pianist from Texas who was studying at the San Francisco Conservatory of Music. Alice thought Opal Perkins would be just the right girl for her favourite youngest brother Stanley, so she invited her home to meet him, and to her great joy, they fell for each other and ended up getting married! Opal was a fine pianist, and often played with the city's leading string quartet. It was thanks to her that I studied in later years with the French composer Darius Milhaud.

Alice had become interested in Chinese art, and later when she was left some money, she thought she would use it to go back to China to study. Her hidebound elder brother Henry, however, tried very hard to stop her. 'You're forty,' he said, 'and you're obviously not going to get married, so you must put that money in the bank so that you will have something to support you in your old age.'

But Alice persisted, and her Christian Science practitioner not only prayed that God would guide her, but he also asked an American couple he knew in Yokohama to meet her ship when it stopped there for three days en route to Shanghai. The kind couple were waiting at the pier when the ship arrived, and took Alice for a drive to show her the sights, including

Yokohama's Sankei-en, the beautiful park whose name means 'Garden of Three Glens'. On the way back, via Zenma village in Isogo on the town's outskirts, they approached a small Western-style house, and the husband said: 'It's tea-time, and Mr Britton's an Englishman. Maybe he'll give us a cup of tea!'

'Mr Britton' not only gave them a cup of tea, but it was love at first sight! He had a delightful little garden, and Mother told me that when she greatly admired a bed of Canterbury Bells, he started to pick her some, then realized it had rained and they would be muddy. But Alice said 'Oh, that's alright, I'll wash them,' which touched him deeply. Frank and Alice had much in common. They were both amateur musicians, loved travel, and had read lots of the same travel books, and were getting along so famously that the couple, who lived up on The Bluff, invited Frank to join them for dinner, after which they all had fun around the piano singing while Alice played the accompaniments.

Next day was Sunday and Frank invited Alice to go for a drive to Kamakura. While they picnicked, he proposed – having known her only four hours! And before the ship sailed for Shanghai two days later, she said 'Yes'!

Alice had to go on to Shanghai, not only because of her luggage on board, but she had been commissioned by Gumps, the well-known San Francisco gifts and home décor store, to buy some Chinese artifacts for them, and so she was obliged to carry out at least some of that commission. The early twentieth-century Chinese rosewood set of quartetto tables here in Hayama in my drawing-room, were bought by her for her new home at the same time!

Besides that, Alice had been invited to spend some time in Shanghai with her childhood friend from Alameda days, Ruth Shreve, whose husband, Benjamin Haile, was there as manager for the Far East of the Pacific Mail Steamship Company. When they found she was to be married, and after Frank duly arrived, they arranged for it to take place in the English cathedral on 15 July 1920, after first registering the marriage at the British Consulate. After the service Ruth strewed white gardenia petals in front of the pair as they came down the cathedral aisle. 'It was beautiful,' wrote Alice as well as describing the lovely reception given to them by the Hailes. When Frank and Alice returned together to Yokohama, and Alice's elder brother heard the news, he cabled his sister: 'Have you lost your mind? Marrying a *foreigner* in a heathen land!' But to Alice, it was a dream marriage, in a fairytale land.

CHAPTER 3

My Father

✦

FRANK GUYVER BRITTON was born on 10 May 1879 in Liverpool, but moved quite soon to Elmdon, near Thaxted in Essex, when his father John inherited the family inn with a farm. Frank thrived amid the beautiful natural surroundings, happily climbing trees and collecting bird's eggs. But his real love was music. As a very small boy he helped the organist at church by working the bellows, in the course of which he managed to work out how to play the instrument, and by the age of twelve he was regularly filling in for the organist.

Frank was only about ten when his mother 'Lizzie' died. Elizabeth Sarah was one of the three Daniels sisters of Littleton Drew in Wiltshire, a beautiful town in the lovely green English countryside. But her elder sister Amelia Jane ('Millie') decided that living in a country inn that was also a public house, with a yeoman farmer father who probably drank heavily and certainly disapproved of Frank's cultural bent, was no place for her talented young nephew so she took him off to London.

Millie Daniels was married to Alfred James Bannister, whose ancestor Captain Samuel Wallis RN, of Corsham Court, near Bath, discovered Tahiti in 1767. Alfred Bannister, artist and calligrapher, was an important influence on Frank's upbringing. Alfred was the son of a cellist and member of the Sacred Harmonic Society, who had sung in the first performance of Mendelssohn's *Elijah* at the Exeter Hall in London, conducted by the composer himself. Their house in Sydenham, south-east London, near Crystal Palace, had a fine library. Frank devoured the books and set about learning to play Alfred's father's cello that stood in one corner, as well as the piano which was also there. It was an environment much to his liking. As a child in the organ loft in Elmdon Frank had been intrigued by the mechanics of the instrument, and it was not long before he took the piano apart in Sydenham and taught himself how to tune it. He graduated as a mechanical engineer in 1904 from the City College of London, and later became a member of the Institution of Mechanical Engineers and the Institute of Metals.

Frank enjoyed books on history, exploration and travel, and was intrigued by what he learned about Japan, especially about William Adams, the first Englishman in Japan. When he heard that the Japanese Shipping line NYK (Nippon Yusen Kaisha) was looking for engineers, he decided to try his luck with them. The Russo-Japanese War was in full swing, which whetted his youthful eagerness for adventure.

He set sail for Japan in the *Sado Maru* in 1904, via the Cape of Good Hope, under sealed orders. Captain O.A. Cowin, its skipper, became a dear friend and later my godfather, though I never met him. The Chief Engineer was also an Englishman, by the name of Kerr. But when they reached the port of Shimonoseki in Japan, Frank was transferred to the *Shinano Maru* as Chief Engineer. The skipper was Captain John Salter. Frank was lucky to have left the *Sado Maru*, for she was torpedoed the very next day. Kerr and three other British officers were rescued, but spent eighteen months in Moscow as prisoners of war.

The *Shinano Maru* had been converted to act as an auxiliary cruiser, or large merchant ship scout, and played a crucial role in the famous Battle of Tsushima in May 1905. Captain Narukawa of the Imperial Japanese Navy was put aboard as naval liaison officer, and, together with fifteen other similarly converted merchant vessels, she was assigned to a numbered square within the Tsushima Straits between Korea and Japan, with orders to report any sighting of the Russian Baltic fleet to Admiral Togo on his flagship, the *Mikasa*. It was the *Shinano Maru* that subsequently made history by its signal on 27 May, at 4.45 am: 'Enemy is in Square 203'. The *Shinano Maru* was capable of speed, and possessed a powerful wireless apparatus. Afterwards, Captain Salter and Frank Britton both received the Asahi Medal for their part in the Russo-Japanese War.

After the end of the war, Frank made seven voyages to the Ogasawara Islands, known then as the Bonin (uninhabited) Islands. In a letter to his uncle in Sydenham, Frank wrote that the Bonin Islanders – descendants of early Western whalers:

> ... will be very sorry when we are taken out of the ship as we are the only fresh Western faces they see, and we always do our best to cheer them up. One trip we brought down a gramophone and another time a magic lantern. They are a very good-hearted lot of people. One old man seventy years of age remembers Commodore Perry calling at the islands some fifty years ago.

Once, on the outward voyage, Frank's ship dropped off a Japanese census-taker on a small island, and when they went back to collect him, the island was nowhere to be found. There was only a huge mass of floating pumice surrounding a few rocky outcrops. The island which the unfortunate census-taker visited may possibly have been one of the 'short-lived islands' comprising the tip of the undersea volcano called Myojin-sho, also known as Bayonnaise Rocks, and designated 'Izu Islands No. 81' in a 1925 survey. It erupted again in 1952. And another island appeared in 2013, and is getting bigger and bigger! Maybe it is the census one back again! Kyodo News now reports that it has joined the island in the Ogasawara chain called Nishinoshima, and that as a result the boundary line of Japan's EEZ (exclusive economic zone) is likely to expand a little.

Frank Britton finally decided to give up seafaring and remain in Japan. Engineers were in great demand. The NYK had been the only source of supply and Frank was the last non-Japanese engineer to be engaged by them, and only a few chiefs were still left in their employ and no juniors.

After leaving NYK, Frank first accepted a position as manager of the Yokohama Engine and Iron Works in the centre of Yokohama beside one of the creeks, set up by an Irishman named Edward Kildoyle. But, in 1906, Britton resigned to become manager of the Zemma Works built in 1900 in the village of Zen-ma in the town of Isogo, on Tokyo Bay on the outskirts of Yokohama.

The shareholders planned to reclaim land and enlarge the operation. In view of the coming 1911 Revision of the Tariff Treaty that would put prohibitive duties on foreign goods, they began negotiations with Babcock and Wilcox, the world's foremost maker of ship's boilers, to make boilers there instead of importing them. The upshot was that in

1910 Babcock took over the Zemma Works, and Frank eventually became Managing Director, Far East, of what was then the biggest foreign business in Japan. Due to Frank's foresight, in 1930 they merged with Mitsui Bussan to become Toyo Babcock, leading to the post-war Babcock Hitachi that it is today.

In his younger days, Frank Britton took long walking trips, became fluent in the spoken language, and came to have a great faith and belief in Japan, for whose people and culture he developed a deep and sympathetic understanding.

Frank was very conscientious and worked tirelessly, all the rest of his life, for Babcock, England and Japan. His 300 workers adored him. He knew the names of each one personally and they came to him with their problems and looked upon him as a father. He never uttered a word of anger to his men. The secret of his remarkable forbearance is revealed in a letter to his uncle in 1909 when Babcock & Wilcox were first considering taking over the Zemma Works. He wrote:

If B&W bring out their own men it is doubtful if they can get on with or even stand the ways of the Japanese. I am irritated sometimes to such a point that I feel like giving them a good English thrashing, and to ensure keeping my temper I always keep cigars on me, and when I feel I cannot control myself any longer I light a cigar and reflect that if one lives in a foreign country one must put up with foreign ways. A cigar is the finest thing in the world to soothe the nerves, and I am quite sure cigars have saved my life many times over, for, without them, I should have struck some of the workmen with the result that the whole works would have been on to me like one man – not an uncommon occurrence in Japan.

When the First World War broke out in August 1914, Frank was one of the first at the British Consulate wanting to enlist, but he was ordered to stay and make munitions for the war, in which Japan was Britain's ally. He ran the works day and night, contenting himself with 'getting at the Boches indirectly if not with cold steel'. He did not forget the need for good public relations, and even designed and organized a march by his workers dressed like bombs! I forget what occasion the march was for.

Skilled at designing, he was also an inventor. He registered many patents, including a portable mudguard to be hung beside motor car wheels to prevent them drenching kimono-clad pedestrians on rainy days! It was very popular. And when gramophones were introduced, he did much for the local industry, devising useful improvements.

CHAPTER 4

How Marrying
Changes My Father's Life

✦

WHEN ALICE HILLER dropped in for tea that day in
1920, Frank was still a bachelor. In one of his letters
to his uncle he writes:

> I control these Works with its 300 employees, and
> keep the company's books as evening amusement,
> so you can see that I have no time to burn on social
> repartee.

Frank did finally manage to obtain an accountant, a delightful Scot called Tom Chisholm, to take some of the burden off his hands. He had also told his uncle that the girls on The Bluff seemed to have little time for engineers. But my mother used to marvel why he had not married beautiful Elizabeth Keith the artist, who was the sister of the wife of his friend journalist John Robertson Scott. Famous for her wood-block prints of Japan and Korea, Elizabeth remained a good family friend of ours.

Frank lived across the road from the Zemma Works and in the interim between marrying Alice in Shanghai and bringing her back with him to Japan, Frank had the house enlarged and beautifully improved. He resisted moving up to The Bluff where all the foreigners lived. Feeling privileged to be in Japan, he refused to live in that completely Western enclave where in those days no one socialized with the Japanese or learned to speak their language. I believe many people thought we were rather peculiar.

While enlarging his house, Frank heard that the *Shinano Maru* was being decommissioned, and so he bought the nostalgic teak of its decks and used the wood, cut into small fish-scale-shaped pieces, imbricated and dyed a beautiful rose colour with the traditional Japanese persimmon juice wood preservative, to cover the sides of the house, He also used the *Shinano Maru* deck teak for our mantelpieces, not only in Yokohama, but later here in Hayama, where our original east side veranda, facing down the beach, was also made of that nostalgic teak.

The Brittons' first child, a son, was alas, stillborn — which my mother was convinced must have been the result of the visit by the accountant's wife who had a frightful cold, which brought on Mother's chronic all-night coughing. That is why I have always felt strongly about the necessity of people with colds staying home, no matter how important their reason for travel might be.

When pregnant with me, Mother sent for her young sister Dorothy, who obtained a job as secretary with the Tokyo YWCA. She was a delightful girl, ten years Mother's junior, who had driven ambulances in France in the First World War. I have a lovely photo of her with kimono-clad one-year-old me (see pl. 5), taken in June amongst the hydrangeas of our garden just four months before the Great Kanto Earthquake which took place on 1 September 1923.

CHAPTER 5

The Great Kanto Earthquake

✦

AUNTIE DOROTHY DID not have to work that Saturday morning of 1 September, but the YWCA telephoned and asked her to go in by tram to the Yokohama post office to send an important cable to their headquarters in America. Apparently, at the post office she met a YWCA colleague, who was there to pick up a fruit cake her mother had sent her for her birthday, by sea mail from the USA. Edith Lacy was a very young widow. Apparently, the two girls then took a rickshaw to a new confectionery shop called Meidi-ya (still spelt that way although it is pronounced Meiji-ya!). They may possibly have wanted to buy some chocolates for Edith's birthday, as well as for a tea party Dorothy had planned for some Tokyo colleagues that afternoon. But just as they got to the Main Street shop, the shaking began, and the rickshaw man, his vehicle and two passengers were crushed beneath the tons of heavy masonry of that handsome modern building. It would be weeks before my father finally found their remains.

Having estimated that a big earthquake was due, Frank had carefully studied the effects of small ones. He had particularly noted their whiplash effect on a brick wall. So he had strengthened his factory walls, buildings and chimneys with steel bolts and bands, as well as the chimney of his home so it would not fall and injure the neighbours.

I was only sixteen months old when the earthquake struck. Frank and Alice had originally been planning to leave Yokohama that morning on a sort of delayed honeymoon in the mountains of Hakone. However, the previous night, after dining with friends at the ill-fated Cherry Mount Hotel, situated part way down a road called Sakura-yama (cherry-tree hill), leading from The Bluff towards the Motomachi shopping street below, they were sipping their coffee and liqueurs on the terrace facing away from the harbour towards the hills. Suddenly, a strange phenomenon caught Frank's attention: he witnessed bolts of peculiar 'upward lightning' coming from the ground and branching out into the sky, like trees. It worried Frank so much that he insisted they leave, although it was still early. At home, their bags were already packed and ready at the front door for the early morning start they intended to make, but fortunately he cancelled the planned trip.

Next day, Saturday, Frank Britton and Tom Chisholm, his Scottish accountant, were together in the office having closed the safe early, a little before twelve. Noon was the normal time for closing safes, and consequently most companies lost all their documents. Frank said: 'When the earthquake comes that is going to destroy Yokohama, I propose that we hang onto the gantry crane. The stairs will go, but the crane will stand.' The words were no sooner out of his mouth than the shaking began, with a great roaring, at exactly two minutes to twelve. 'I didn't know it was coming so soon,' said Chisholm, 'I'm going down the stairs while they last.' Frank lost faith in his own plan and followed suit, more or less thrown down the stairs, for it was impossible to stand. Once down, they could only crawl. At the gate Frank turned and saw that a cornice had landed over their path like a protective cover from the flying debris, placed by a guardian angel. They carried on across the road to Frank's house and stood up, facing each other. 'There goes Yokohama!' said Frank looking across Tom Chisholm's shoulder at the great cloud of dust enveloping the city. 'And there goes Yokosuka!' said Tom, looking in the opposite direction. In spite of his slight limp, Chisholm hurried off on foot towards Negishi and The Bluff to see what had happened to his wife and young son. They were killed, and his home demolished.

Frank went into our house to see if Alice and the baby were all right. Alice had been in the kitchen where the stove had broken apart, setting fire to the tea-towels hanging above it. They put out the fire as soon as she and the cook could stand, and Alice struggled up the stairs to the nursery, which was a shambles, with heavy globs of wall plaster jumbled in a heap where the baby's high chair had been. To her great relief she heard the voice of Kin-san, my nanny: 'We're here Madam, under the bed.' Kin-san told Alice she could see out into the garden as the space between walls and floor kept opening and shutting. The frame of the house had stood, thanks to Frank's reinforcing. As aftershocks kept coming, Alice's first words to Frank were a frantic, 'Find sister Dorothy!' as Frank disappeared.

There was a strong wind, and soon Alice was aware of an ominous crackling as a high wall of smoke and flames headed their way. It was terrifying, and she wondered if it was the end of the world. Fires had broken out all over the city. It was lunchtime, and thousands of broken charcoal-burning stoves had set the wooden houses alight. After what seemed an age, the wall of fire miraculously stopped advancing. Eventually, Frank returned, exhausted, clothes singed and reeking of smoke, too tired to explain. It transpired that as a result of Frank's courageous example and efforts, the fire had been brought under control and finally put out after only fifty houses had burned. He had climbed up himself onto burning roofs and organized bucket brigades with water from the nearby canal, and they had managed to demolish enough houses to make a wide path across which the fire could not leap.

Almost the whole of Yokohama burned to the ground, but thanks to Frank, Isogo was saved, and became a place of refuge for thousands. Later, the grateful citizens got together a petition to have his efforts appropriately recognized, but he was so modest that he stopped them, saying, 'I did no more than any Englishman would do.'

After spending a few nights in the garden, rushing into the house in between aftershocks to get necessities, they decided to try and leave. Frank hired a fisherman to row him and Mother and Kin-san and me around the headland of Honmoku into Yokohama harbour, where several steamships were standing by. The P&O *Dongola* was just about to weigh anchor. Frank called up to a man in the bow: 'Can you take us aboard?' They agreed, and we managed to climb up the remaining narrow gangway. We found that it was mostly the badly injured foreigners who were on board, but Alice's sister was not among them. Frank had hoped against hope to find her there. Landing at Kobe, Frank settled us at the Miyako Hotel, in Kyoto, and returned to Yokohama by train with medical supplies and food for his men. He quickly got the factory going again so that the workmen could have employment. He also persuaded the Japanese navy to bring up timber by destroyer from Shizuoka, and with this he organized the speedy building of a temporary British Consulate.

Frank never stopped looking for his sister-in-law. After weeks of harrowing and gruesome search, he finally found her unrecognizable remains – with those of her friend Edith Lacy – crushed flat together in the rickshaw under tons of masonry, identifiable only by Alice's bank book and Edith's hat, which were found nearby. The two girls are buried together in the Yokohama Foreign General Cemetery, and since war's end the YWCA have held an annual memorial service at their grave on 1 September.

For those weeks after the earthquake, mother and toddler and nanny found comfort in beautiful, historical Kyoto, where famed missionary, Mary Florence Denton, one of the founders of Doshisha College, and its first president, so kindly took us under her wing. During that time, Frank, together with the now widowed Tom Chisholm, lived in our house, shaken but standing, which they shared with a contingent of military police – *kempeitai* – on security duty in view of the nearby prison whose criminals had escaped, and the spreading, though unfounded, rumours of rioting Koreans.

CHAPTER 6

Hayama

✦

WHEN MY NANNY Kin-san – whom I called Ten-ten – and Mother and I came back about a month later from Kyoto, Daddy rented a house for us at the seaside in Hayama, and my earliest memory is of the scary rugged drive from Isogo in the back of a lorry. I also remember we were not allowed to sound our motor car horn in Hayama because Yoshihito, the Taisho Emperor, was lying ill in the Imperial Villa Annex. And I remember, too, the tragedy for me of falling into a mud puddle and ruining a lovely new outfit my great aunt in Oregon had sent me! It kept

me wondering for years as to where it had happened. Believe it or not, the puddle was still there, when back in post-war Japan in the 1950s I came upon it suddenly, up a little lane, giving me a curious feeling of having come full circle!

The house we rented was at the top of a steep flight of steps from the beach. English friends of ours had spent the summer there, and were having a pre-prandial drink on the lawn on that day, 1 September 1923, when the earth began to shake and the seawater suddenly receded, revealing unfamiliar rocks and leaping fish, before coming back in three long heaves, hurling great waves up against the walls of the royal villas. 'GONE TO THE HILLS'. The message our friends had scratched on the wood of the front door was still there when I came back to Japan in 1949. Fortunately, that particular tsunami reached no higher than the garden, which was about 17 feet above sea level.

As I write this, three years after the magnitude nine Great Tohoku Earthquake of 2011, I am still overcome with sympathy for the victims of that even worse disaster. Those enormous tsunamis swept away town after town and thousands of people on Japan's north-eastern coast. Thinking about their ordeal, I have finally understood, after all these years, why my father could not bear to look at a doll I had once made which my mother had forced me to hide away, out of his sight. It hurt my feelings at the time. I had never received an advertised 'walking doll' my parents had tried to order for me, a small lonely only-child, and

when I was a little bigger I had tried to make a doll my size to keep me company. But it was so badly made, that its ugly face and straggly hair must have reminded my Father of all the gruesome corpses he had seen when searching for my Auntie Dorothy's remains!

That 'GONE TO THE HILLS' house was leased to missionaries, and had a tiny organ, which I tried to play and found great fun. But there were ghosts, too: one night two scary little dogs appeared on my bed. My screaming woke my parents, who assured me there was nothing there at all. But I can still see them clearly in my mind even now. Two little dogs like the ones you see in old Japanese prints. The servants were sure it was because I was born in the Year of the Dog, and they planted tiny red flags all around the house to keep them away.

The missionaries wanted us out by Christmas, which my mother thought rather un-Christian of them, seeing that we were earthquake refugees, but fortunately we managed to find another house to rent. It was next to the park that was right beside the Imperial Villa, and we had it for a couple of years as our beach house.

We enjoyed life in Hayama by the sea, and one day at the local railway station, Mother made friends with a lovely Japanese lady who spoke perfect English. When they discovered they each had a little girl the same age – both not quite two – they determined that we should meet. But to their amazement, they found we were already bosom friends, playing

together down on the beach, watched over by
our nannies! Wakako Okubo became my oldest
and dearest friend. She was the granddaughter of
historically famous Toshimichi Okubo who played
an important part in the Meiji Restoration and the
opening up of Japan.

The island country had been closed to the world for
over two hundred years, from 1638 to 1868. There
had been an emperor, of continuous direct descent,
based in Kyoto since time immemorial. But in 1192,
the then Emperor ennobled a clan leader for fighting
the aboriginal Ainu, and called him Shogun, meaning
Barbarian Subduing Commander-in-Chief. This first
Shogun went on to establish a military government
which came to be known as the Shogunate.

The Shogunate took over Kamakura as their base,
but eventually, the greatest Shogun of them all,
Tokugawa Ieyasu, set up his capital in Edo, now known
as Tokyo, and established such a tightly-controlled,
fool-proof régime that his family held the seat of
power for almost 300 years. To minimize the possi-
bility of his vassal feudal lords rising against him, he
required them to maintain residences in Edo as well as
in their home fiefs, and to live in their Edo residences
for several months each year, as well as leaving their
wives and families in Edo as hostages at all times.
Barriers were set up throughout the country, and all
travellers were searched. Guards were always on the
lookout for 'arms coming into Edo and women going
out', and gatherings of more than a few people at any
time without a permit were forbidden.

But as time went on another threat emerged. In the sixteenth century many Jesuit missionaries began coming to Japan, and the Japanese people converted to Christianity in droves. Then came Spanish and Portuguese traders, who were at first well received. Ieyasu, however, noted that Spain and Portugal were in the process of building up for themselves a sizeable empire in the Far East, and it occurred to him that the missionaries and the traders might be the thin edge of the wedge for an eventual conquest of Japan.

This threat may well have been first pointed out to the astute Shogun by a unique member of his court, that Englishman named William Adams – the first Briton ever to set foot on Japanese soil. He was a ship's navigator who was shipwrecked and stranded in Japan in 1600, and became the trusted confidant of the Shogun, who kept him in Japan and made him a Japanese nobleman. From Adams, the Shogun learned much about Elizabethan England including the arts of navigation and shipbuilding, as well as some contemporary world geography and the state of affairs that existed between the European political powers.

As time went on, the Japanese government came to view Christianity as a subversive force within Japan, just as Communism does to certain democratic Western powers today. Unsurprisingly, some years after the death of Adams and Ieyasu, the Shogun's son decided to take no chances with the foreigners. All Christians were ruthlessly exterminated (1637–1638) and no one was allowed in or out of Japan. All contact with the outside world was stopped, except for a

small amount of business with China and a tiny Dutch trading post on a small, closely-guarded man-made island (Deshima) in Nagasaki harbour. This state of affairs went on for over two hundred years, until 1853 when America sent Commodore Matthew Perry with a fleet of naval vessels to force Japan to admit trade, and allow the refuelling of passing American whaling ships.

This proved a golden opportunity for the anti-Shogunate *daimyo*, the feudal samurai lords in Japan. Then finally, in 1868, ten years after the Shogun signed a commercial treaty with the United States, the Tokugawa military regime was overthrown by a royalist force which brought the Emperor up to Edo, changed the name of the city to Tokyo, and set up an enlightened government modelled on those of Europe.

Samurais of Satsuma (now called Kagoshima) were the prime movers, led by Takamori Saigo and Toshimichi Okubo, grandfather of my best friend Wakako. Okubo and Saigo went on to strongly advise and influence the new boy emperor Mutsuhito, better known by his reign name Meiji, and in 1871 Okubo joined three others in the major Iwakura diplomatic mission to the USA, Britain and Europe in which they spent a year and a half amassing knowledge of the outside world.

While they were away, Japan experienced very troubled times in its endeavour to marry the old with the new; various rebellions took place, including a tragic one within Okubo's own Satsuma fief, which was

being governed by Saigo, who eventually committed suicide, and Okubo, my friend's grandfather, on his return from abroad was assassinated. He was not the only member of Wakako's family to come to a tragic end. Her mother was the daughter of Prime Minister, and later Finance Minister Takahashi, who was murdered in the 26 February 1936, attacked by anti-government junior army officers, when three cabinet ministers were killed. The story of this remarkable man is told in Richard J. Smethurst's *From Foot Soldier to Finance Minister: Takahashi Korekiyo, Japan's Keynes* (Harvard University Press, 2007). He had learned to speak fluent English, and was very friendly with American financier Jacob Schiff, who invited Takahashi's daughter to stay with them while she studied at a US college. That was why she spoke English so well when she met my mother at the railway station soon after the earthquake. Takahashi sent his son to Oxford, who returned with a ravishingly beautiful bride he met during a holiday in Berlin. Anita, my dear friend Wakako's young German aunt, became a close friend of ours post-war, when she lived in the house next door to us.

In those early days in Japan, mixed marriages were looked at askance and poor Anita's marriage was forced apart, and she eventually married a German businessman. But she told me that young Takahashi was the true love of her life, in spite of some interesting love affairs she had later with visitors to Tokyo's Western community, including a famous

violinist. She told me she thought of each as a separate cherished drawer in her heart!

Statesman and diplomat Count Munemitsu Mutsu was so opposed to his son marrying an English girl he met while at Cambridge, that they had to wait seventeen anguished years before managing to tie the knot, after which the Countess wrote that classic book entitled *Kamakura, Fact and Legend.* Similar cases abound in that era. But since the war I am happy to say mixed marriages in Japan are now so frequent that a club called the Association of Foreign Wives of Japanese is a splendid ever-growing organization. As a teenager, watching pale-skinned women on various country's beaches trying to acquire a healthy tan, I used to wish that inter-marriage would go on apace and produce a *café-au-lait* world, so that there would be no more racism at all anywhere!

CHAPTER 7

Mother Contacts
Her First Japanese Friend

✦

ONE OF THE first things my mother did after marrying
and settling in Yokohama, was to get in touch
with Suzu Numano, her very first Japanese friend.
Mrs Numano was now back in Japan, a widow,
with her son and two school-age daughters Sumié
and Chié. After moving to Portland, Oregon,
from San Francisco, the handsome young Japanese
consul-general had tragically died of pneumonia
from a germ caught on a consular trip to China. Mrs
Numano visited us several times in Hayama, and when

we were back in Yokohama, the day she brought her two daughters to tea remains very clearly etched in my memory. That is probably because I disgraced myself. The four of them had tea on a bridge table set up in my nursery, covered with a beautifully embroidered Chinese tablecloth which my mother had bought in China. I was very small, and was underneath the table playing on the floor with a set of wooden letters of the alphabet. All I could see of our guests was the lower part of Mrs Numano's elegant silk kimono, and the legs of her two girls in their school uniform black stockings. In the midst of their nostalgic conversation about San Francisco days, Mother suddenly discovered that I had cut out an 'A' from her precious table-cloth, using scissors and the alphabet letter. All hell broke loose. I even made it worse by blaming the nefarious act on Isabella, my doll.

But in spite of my naughtiness, dear Mrs Numano, bless her, was very taken with me as a child, and was particularly fascinated with my bilinguality, and used to tell people I was really Japanese, and just had a Western skin! Suzu and her family have remained very dear friends. One day in the 1960s she rang my mother to say that her grandson had married a Welsh girl, in Greece, and that the young newly-weds would be living in her Nagashima son-in-law's handsome beach villa in nearby Zushi, and she hoped we would become friends.

We liked Hayama so much in those post-earthquake years, that in 1925 my father leased a small piece of land – a rock with a fisherman's shack on it. In place

of the shack he had a house built, which he designed combining both Western and Japanese features, a mere biscuit toss, as he used to say, from the sea. Isshiki beach was not crowded like those in Kamakura, Zushi and Morito, for it was too far to walk from Zushi station, and the only transport was a small horse-drawn carriage holding eight passengers, so only people with cars had villas there in those days, and were mostly aristocrats and royalty.

In 1926, when we moved into our new beach house, the Taisho Emperor died, and was succeeded by the Showa Emperor, Hirohito. The ceremony of succession took place in the Imperial Villa Annex, which was just along the road from us, and I remember watching a ceremonial procession go by, past our house, and how impressed I was by the quartet of handsome black oxen drawing a beautiful ancient carriage belonging to the local Shinto shrine.

From our house it was a short walk up a lane to the Okubo's house on the hillside, and I'll never forget the day I was old enough to walk there to play without my nanny. When I left to walk home, Mrs Okubo said in English, 'Please give your mother my love'. I worried and worried all the way back, trying to figure out how one gave a person somebody's love. I still recall the agony whenever I walk on that hillside lane.

Another memory that still recurs without fail on that lane is the walking doll I wanted so badly. One November evening, after I had been put to bed, I could not sleep and crept downstairs, where I found

my parents busy poring over an enormous Sears, Roebuck mail order catalogue. Obviously, they had wanted to keep it a surprise, but I could not help seeing the fascinating illustration, and I discovered that they were planning to order for me for Christmas a large 'walking doll'. I was absolutely thrilled, and could hardly wait for it to arrive. But alas, it never did. I never learned the reason, but being a lonely only child, I went on for years picturing that companion as I walked to the Okubo's and back. Little did I know that years later it would eventually materialize!

CHAPTER 8

Royal Friends

✦

ONE DAY ON the beach, some young princesses asked me to join them in an intriguing game called *jindori* (land grabbing). First you draw a largish area on the sand, where the winner of the traditional *janken* (scissors-paper-stone) choice-deciding fist-toss, semi-circles a portion – with stationary thumb and moving forefinger – to start a 'battle encampment'. When the whole area is filled, the player with the largest camp-site wins. It was a popular game with Japanese children in those days. On arriving home I was surprised to find my mother furious. She had been watching us from a

distance. 'How dare you teach that disgusting game to princesses,' she said. It was the 'scissors-paper-stone' part she objected to. She thought that it was only used at geisha parties my father had told her about, where the loser has to take off an item of clothing!

The Dowager Princess Kitashirakawa and her daughters lived in a large, beautiful estate – complete with a handsome thatched-roof gate – next door to Wakako's maternal grandfather Takahashi's villa, both located just along the road from us. The Kitashirakawas became lifelong friends too. Before the war our friendship only took place on the beach, but after the war, we saw them often, because royals who were not immediate members of the Imperial Family had to become more or less the same as commoners. The older sister, Princess Sawa, who was married to a high-ranking chamberlain, regularly came to my house for the rest of her life as a member of my bridge foursome, which included Wakako Okubo too.

Not long ago, I asked Princess Sawa if her younger sister had spoken to me that day years ago when we were children, because they had perhaps heard about me from Wakako's unmarried aunt, Miss Okubo, who happened to be their lady-in-waiting. But she said 'Oh no! She just liked your looks and wanted to be friends with you!' I had been playing alone on the sand in front of our house that day when the Kitashirakawas came by. They stopped, and the younger Princess Taé asked me what my name was. I told her, and then asked *her* name. 'Taé' she said. To me it sounded like *tai* (bream) so I asked her why she

was called 'bream', and she replied that it was because she looked like one! She had a great sense of humour. Taé-sama very sadly died of a heart attack not long after we met again. She had married a Tokugawa of the former shogun's family. Their father, Prince Kitashirakawa had lived in Paris with his bride as a young man. He had an honorary position at the Japanese Embassy. Later, very sadly, he lost his life in Paris in a motor car accident, while driving. There is a monument marking the place, and the surviving widowed dowager princess walked with a bad limp. Princess Fusako Kitashirakawa was the daughter of the Meiji Emperor, and as an Emperor's widowed daughter she held the position of Chief High Priestess of Shinto's supreme shrine, in Ise. Established 2,000 years ago, it is rebuilt every twenty years.

One Christmas not so long ago, my mother wanted to learn the phrase Japanese people habitually use when they give someone a gift. My mother was not a linguist, and did not speak Japanese, but she was good at memorizing, so she said just write it down and let me memorize it. But I forgot to tell her what it meant, which was remiss of me. The Japanese are always very humble in referring to anything concerning themselves, and when they give a gift they call it a worthless, insignificant and trifling thing, whereas we imply it is 'something nice we think you will like'. My mother was successful all that Christmas long in giving 'insignificant, worthless gifts' to her Japanese friends. And then much later, in the following spring, the Dowager Princess and her elder

daughter Sawa-sama came for tea, and she handed Mother a gift, saying, 'This belonged to my father'. My mother knew her father was Emperor Meiji, and in her excitement, all she could think of saying was that phrase I had taught her, but before she got to the 'trifling and worthless' part, I managed to knock a priceless Crown Derby cup we had off the tea-table and cause an effective distraction!

'Trifling' reminds me of my own new special recipe for Trifle, which my dear friend Carmen Blacker thought was delicious, and suggested it be called 'Kitashirakawa Surprise'. It came about because I had been asked to appear on a TV programme which featured artists, writers, musicians, etc., who were invited to make their favourite dish. I decided to do a Trifle, because I thought it was probably easy. But I am not much of a cook and did not realize how difficult custard could be. Bird's Custard was unavailable in Japan, and try as I might, mine always curdled. But it was alright at the studio, because it is apparently the custom for a professional to make the same thing, to show at the end in case there is time-consuming cooking involved – or if one's own is not up to scratch! Next day, who should appear at the door but the Kitashirakawas – mother and daughter – wanting me to show them how to make that dessert which looked so good and so easy. I was baffled! In desperation, I explained the general idea and then got them to stay in the drawing room with my mother while I tried to sort something out in the kitchen with what I could find in the fridge. The result was superb.

Far better, I still think, than regular English Trifle! My base is an immensely popular Japanese sponge cake called *kasutera,* from *pao de Castella* (Castile bread) which was brought to Japan by the Portuguese in the sixteenth century. On it I dribble *ume-shu* (Japanese plum wine), then cover it with cut-up strawberries and kiwi-fruit, and top it with yoghurt – tasty and much healthier than custard!

In the old pre-war days we were almost the only foreigners in Hayama. Most of the Westerners on The Bluff in Yokohama spent their summers in Karuizawa and Nojiri, mountain resorts which were then mainly foreign enclaves too. So my summer friends were all Japanese. They were mostly members of the royalty and aristocracy. Right opposite our house was the villa of Baron Takuma Dan, the head of Mitsui, who had recently been murdered by extremists for promoting friendship with England. His daughter Mrs Ogura, with three lovely daughters, had a house in Baron Dan's enormous garden. Next door to them was the villa of Count Kentaro Kaneko, who wrote Japan's pre-war Constitution. Diagonally across the road from us was the summer villa of the Kajima Corporation, one of Japan's leading construction companies. The director's niece Nanako was one of my friends, too. Their extensive houses and gardens, all among the hills on the opposite side of the road, were wonderful settings for our games of hide and seek. I introduced that Western version called 'sardines', in which the seekers get in with the hider and the last seeker loses.

It became very popular, and it was once when all we children crowded into a Japanese futon closet at the Ogura's that I first noticed the Baron's cute little grandson Ikuma, two years younger than I was, who became one of Japan's leading composers.

We all had great fun together, but only in the afternoons, for Japanese children are busy doing homework all morning, even in the summer holidays. That is why there is virtually no illiteracy in Japan. So, in the early part of the day, my companions were the ocean and its fascinating denizens. The sea was a wonderful friend. It was always there for me, and it put its arms around me and hugged me whenever I went into it. And it talked to me. Watery words of friendship and love.

And in addition to my friend the sea, there were several families of imaginary people who I imagined living in nice houses in the crevices of the rock in front of our house. I would sometimes invite an imaginary family into our house, and I still remember how real they were to me, and how I once had to stop my mother from sitting down on top of 'somebody'. 'O Mother,' I cried, 'That's Mrs Aroosla sitting there!' The other day I came across a note my darling mother had made of the names of my imaginary friends, and there was a whole family of Arooslas!

One enormous rock rises up out of the sand below our house, to the right, like the prow of a large vessel, which I named The Warship Hotel, and marked with a large sign. My father, of course, lost no time in getting rid of that sign!

Another friend was Mount Fuji. I used to get up very early, while my parents were still asleep, and creep out of the house and down onto the sand, and run along to the rocks at our end of the beach. I would make myself comfortable there on one of the rocks, and gaze for hours across Sagami Bay at the mountain, always radiantly beautiful in the dawn light.

That is how I filled in my mornings while my Japanese friends were busy with their homework.

CHAPTER 9

The Japanese Language

✦

I DO NOT think many Westerners realize how extraordinarily hard Japanese have to work, from the time they are young children, in order to memorize the basic 1,006 kanji – the Chinese whole-word ideograms they are required to learn during their six grades of elementary school. And that is in addition to the two alphabets of fifty-six syllables each, called *kana*, which a Japanese monk invented in the ninth century when Chinese writing was adopted, to enable Japanese people to conjugate verbs and indicate Japanese parts of speech such as particles and prepositions,

because of the great difference between Chinese and Japanese. (See also page 6, note 1.)

One's mind truly boggles to think of all those complicated writing symbols the Japanese people have to cope with, when all *we* have is just one twenty-six-letter alphabet, or two if you separate capitals and small letters. In comparison with theirs, our written language is mere child's play. Those 1,006 basic kanji, which must be mastered in primary school, are just the beginning. In addition to both fifty-six syllable *kana* alphabets, children must finish high school with a knowledge of 1,945 kanji, which is the present post-war figure officially endorsed for current use. In 1946, the government had issued a list of 1,850 characters, recommending that people confine themselves to these. But most newspapers still use about 2,500. And now they hardly ever make use of those helpful tiny *hiragana* that once upon a time were printed alongside difficult kanji indicating their pronunciation.

But it was much worse before the war. Then about 6,000 kanji were in use, and I remember often seeing Japanese gentlemen working out on the palms of their hands, while conversing, what certain kanji were! You do not see that now. Having the number of kanji for current use officially curtailed after the war enables many words now to be spelled out simply in *hiragana*, and many of the remaining kanji have thankfully been simplified. It was the pre-war variety that I later worked so hard to try and learn during some free periods at my English boarding school!

But learning written Japanese still takes a great deal of time, since besides memorizing over 2,000 of those complicated hieroglyphics, there is also the problem as to how they are pronounced. *Kanji* have a far greater variety of pronunciations than our few words that are written the same but pronounced differently. Each kanji has at least two pronunciations – the *kun* or Japanese reading, and the *on* or Chinese-derived reading.

Chinese is to Japanese what Latin is to English. Just as we use Roman letters, the Japanese use Chinese symbols, and just as the English language often has both native Anglo-Saxon words and Greek or Latin-derived words for the same things – for example 'walking' and 'ambulation' – Japanese similarly has both native Japanese words and Chinese-derived words. It is the same sort of connection. And moreover, the British are not a bit like the Italians and Greeks, although they look alike. Similarly, the Chinese and Japanese are not a bit alike in spite of looking more or less the same!

Surprisingly, where our Latin or Greek-derived words are invariably long words in English, the Chinese-derived words are very short in Japanese! Clarity-loving Winston Churchill used to say, 'Don't use a long word where a short word will do,' but strangely enough it is the other way round in Japanese. Long Japanese words are much clearer and easier to understand than the short Chinese-derived words, of which so many sound alike.

Americans tend to use long words more than we do. For instance American stations have signs saying,

RHYTHMS, RITES AND RITUALS

'Expectoration forbidden' while we just have 'Do not spit'! And there was a teacher at my American university who deliberately used long words. Instead of saying, 'Please phone me about it' she would say 'I shall require your telephonic communication'.

The *kana* alphabets invented by those Japanese monks are imperative in making meaning clear. Nouns and verb roots are generally written in kanji with the verb endings, prepositions, etc., added in *kana* script. For instance, here is the kanji for 'walk' 歩, basically read 'aru'. Followed by き, the syllable *ki* in *hiragana*, the word becomes *aruki*, 'walking'. The same kanji followed by 'kô' becomes *hokô*, 'ambulation', the Chinese-derived word for 'walking'. It is just as if we had a picture-word for 'walk', and if you saw X-ing you would read it 'walking', and if you saw X-tion you would automatically know it should be read 'ambulation'. This in itself shows how intellectually challenging written Japanese is!

Before the Second World War many more kanji were used, but now that thankfully the list of kanji has been officially shortened, let us hope that the two *kana* alphabets will be used more and more. It is interesting that the difference between *katakana* and *hiragana* is the same as the difference between the two varieties of our own alphabet – upper and lower case; *katakana*, like our capitals, is angular, whereas *hiragana*, like our small letters, is cursive.

You can see this difference in the Japanese vowels. Notice the different order from ours. The pronunciation is as in: 'But he soon set off.'

A	I	U	E	O		a	i	u	e	o
ア	イ	ウ	エ	オ		あ	い	う	え	お

(*katakana*) (*hiragana*)

Apart from the vowels, the only other single Roman letter sound in the Japanese *kana* alphabet is N (n) ン (ん) as used at the end of a word, because the alphabet is made up of syllables. consisting of the vowel sounds, in that order, preceded by successive consonants in the order K, S, T, N, H, M, Y, R, W, as follows:

KA KI KU KE KO, SA SHI SU SE SO, etc.

Certain syllables do not exist. For instance, SI, instead of which there is SHI. Neither are there any L syllables at all.

The nearest approach to f is the syllable fu.

G, Z, D, B and P syllables are formed by adding diacritical marks to the K, S, T, and H syllabic symbols.

Katakana are almost exclusively used today to spell foreign words and foreign names, for like any growing language, over the years Japanese has taken in a large proportion of words from abroad. Many Dutch and Portuguese words entered the Japanese language hundreds of years ago, such as *pan* from the Portuguese *pao* meaning 'bread', *buriki* from the Dutch *blik*, meaning 'tin', and *koppu* from the Dutch *kopje*, meaning 'a drinking glass', which I keep on mixing up with 'cup'!

In later years, words from other European countries crept in, such as *arubaito* from the German

arbeit (work) which in Japan means 'work on the side', and *abekku* from the French *avec* (with) which has come to mean not just plain 'with' but 'boy with girl' – in other words 'a courting couple'! But the language which has infiltrated Japanese to the greatest extent is the English language, and is going on apace. English has received from Japan a fair number of words itself, such as 'geisha', 'kimono', 'obi', 'samisen', 'kakemono', 'rickshaw', 'tycoon', 'mikado' and 'tsunami', as a glance through any dictionary will show, but the greater debt by far is on the other side. Countless English words are by now well established in the Japanese language, and many have been abbreviated out of all recognition, such as *suto*, which is short for *sutoraiku* (strike), and *biru*, which is short for *birudeingu* (building), the latest being *sumaho* for 'smart phone'!

Foreign words in a Japanese text can always be distinguished by the fact that they are written in *katakana*, which alas, with the paucity of its sounds, is a great hindrance to Japanese learning English. I call it their 'Katakana Prison'.

It is of course possible to write everything in Japanese just using *kana*, but even a few of the beautiful Chinese characters expressing whole words sprinkled through the text make the meaning easier to grasp quickly at a glance, so one hopes they will never be completely abolished. But I hope very much that they will bring back that custom they used a long time ago when Japan was not a hundred per cent literate as they are now. It is called *furigana*, and prints tiny

kana next to difficult kanji for the benefit of people like me who have not memorized them all!

I corresponded happily for years in *romaji* (Roman letters) with Ikuma Dan, both of us writing in Japanese, and I usually write my script that way for Japanese talks and presentations. Words have to be separated, of course, as in English. Takuboku Ishikawa (1886–1912), whom Professor Donald Keene says was 'perhaps the most popular tanka poet who ever lived' wrote a diary in Roman letters, published in 1909. Although they were originally derived from pictures, the Chinese characters, or kanji, have been highly stylized and modified over the centuries. Some resemble the original pictures. 木 is 'tree'. Two of them, 林 is 'a grove', and three, 森 is 'a forest'. 'Fish' is 魚 and that fish character appears as a radical on the left-hand side of every character for the name of a fish. For instance, 鮃 is 'flounder' and 鯉 is 'carp'.

Spoken Japanese is relatively simple from the point of view of grammar. It has even fewer verb forms than English, there are no articles ('a', 'an', 'the', etc.), personal pronouns ('I', 'he', 'you', etc.) are seldom used, and there is no special form for the plural. But this kind of simplicity is more than made up for by the richness in special courteous forms. For example, there are two sets of words in many cases to differentiate between things connected with oneself, one's relatives, and one's employees on the one hand, and the same things connected with others. For instance, the word *haha* means 'my mother' or 'our mother', while if you want to say 'your mother', or wish to refer to the mother of anyone not connected with yourself, you must use *o-kasan* or the even politer *o-kasama*. Where there is not a special word, the honorific 0 is usually just put in front of the word. For instance, *denwa* means 'telephone', but *o-denwa* means 'a telephone call for you' or 'your telephone call'. Verbs, too, have several forms according to courtesy. Besides the ordinary two forms, familiar and polite, of which the familiar, as with French, is mainly used between close relatives and intimate friends, Japanese has a special humble form, which is used when referring to oneself, and an honorific form which is an especially polite way of referring to others. For instance, the ordinary polite way of saying 'go' is *ikimasu*. The humble form, meaning 'I go', is *mairimasu*, and the honorific form, meaning 'you go', or 'he goes', if 'he' is connected with the person one is addressing, is *irasshaimasu*. All this sounds very complicated, but really it is not, and is merely based on the courteous assumption that 'you' and 'yours' are always august and exalted personages, whereas 'I' and 'mine' are very lowly and humble. It is really no different from the idea of respect and consideration for others on which courtesy the world over is based. It is just that the Japanese language provides a sort of ready-made framework which aids and abets courtesy in social intercourse without the need for adjectives. The language makes it an everyday, natural thing for people to be polite to one another without much conscious effort.

CHAPTER 10

Winters in Yokohama

✦

WHILE MY CHILDHOOD summer friends were mostly Japanese, my winter friends were Western children living up on Yokohama's *Yamate,* which the foreigners called The Bluff. Many of them had governesses brought with them from their home countries. For the rest of us there were three schools for English speakers, the Catholic St Maur's for girls, St Joseph's for boys and the non-denominational Yokohama International School, which I attended for two years. The headmistress was a delightful Canadian lady. I enjoyed her lessons, and there was no homework.

There was one funny episode, however, on account of her Canadian accent. We were having a geography lesson, and I cannot remember what country it was she was describing, but she explained that the industry of that country was chalklit. Putting up my hand, I asked, 'What is chalklit?' All the other children seemed to know what it was, and they all turned around and looked at me in wonderment. 'Haven't you ever had any?' one of them asked. 'No,' I replied. 'What does it look like?' 'Well, it's brown,' said the headmistress. Finally, I realized it was chocolate! I was used to my mother's American pronunciation *chahklet* but *chawklet* sounded as if it was some sort of chalk!

Having reached the International School's limit, the following year I entered St Maur's, where I was given a most unusual assignment by an amazingly imaginative teacher. I have always wondered if she thought it up specially for me. She knew I had done a lot of writing as a child, of stories and plays and poetry, so she asked me to take Shakespeare's *Much Ado About Nothing* in *Lamb's Tales* and rewrite it as a play! It was truly a brilliant assignment, which I enjoyed enormously – except for one great problem. I was twelve, knew nothing about sex, and after much thought had come to the conclusion that it was the priest or vicar's *words* at the marriage ceremony that caused the bride to become pregnant, so I took great pains to avoid a marriage scene! Also around that time, I was spending the day with my three French friends, the daughters of the French Consul, when one of them said 'let's play wedding' and for the same reason

I was terrified, and frantically reiterated *non, non, non,* much to their uncomprehending disappointment.

My parents had been very eager to enrol me in the new Ferris Seminary on The Bluff, where the teachers were mostly Japanese. It was built where the Cherry Mount Hotel used to be, where my parents saw that strange 'tree lightning' that saved our lives in the Great Earthquake. If I had been able to go to Ferris, I could have studied Japanese properly there, as well as music, in which that school has gone from strength to strength. I suppose they decided against a local Japanese school down in Isogo because they were afraid of the bullying I would certainly have been subjected to. But alas, the Ferris Seminary refused to accept me, a foreigner, because they said it had been established by an American missionary organization specifically for the education of Japanese girls.

So I had to make do with private lessons in both Japanese and music. I started piano lessons from a very nice English lady, whose husband was an engineer like Daddy and whose little boy was Daddy's godson, who lay in his pram beside the piano when I had my lessons with his mother. I still remember being at his christening in Yokohama's Christ Church, and how amazed I was by the slight swaying to and fro of the adults towering all around me! Perhaps it was the earthquake that unconsciously made me so sensitive to movement. Daddy really wanted me to become a violinist, because orchestras always needed plenty of them, so work would be easy to obtain. His friend must have also been convinced of that too, because Daddy's godson studied violin when the family returned to England, no doubt with a splendid teacher, and eventually made a successful career in the Oslo Symphony as first second violin.

Unfortunately, the violin teacher my father found for me was not inspiring at all. He never gave me any nice music to play, only *Kaiser's Exercises* – nothing but scales and finger technique. It was like teaching someone a foreign language by starting out with grammar – to my mind, the very worst way. But Jussuf Dermot was an Irishman, with a sense of humour, and did teach me one bit of 'music' which I have never forgotten. He said if I should ever want to get away with swearing, all I needed do was to use the name of Wagner's opera and just say 'Gotterdamerung'!

My Japanese language teacher was another bad choice. She was a charming retired Japanese school mistress, known for her beautiful calligraphy, but her husband worked for my father, and so she was far too polite to be strict with the boss's daughter. She only got as far as teaching me how to write the fifty *katakana*, the easier of the two Japanese syllabaries – but at least she insisted I use a brush and India ink.

One of the things we foreign girls enjoyed on The Bluff was our ballet class taught by Miss Pavlova from the Ballet Russe. She was no relation to the famous Anna Pavlova, who visited Japan when I was still a baby. Pavlov, like our Smith, is a common name in Russia. Our teacher was Elena Pavlova, and her classes took place each week in one of the houses on The Bluff, usually that of the Managing Director of

Shell Oil, known in Japan as the Rising Sun Petro-
leum Company. We used to give performances of
our dances for the benefit of charities such as the
former Ministering Children's League, and usually
performed on the spacious lawns of foreign residences
on The Bluff. Elena and her sister, who was also a
ballerina, were refugees from the Soviet Revolution.
They built a house in Kamakura on a hill overlooking
the sea and had a great many Japanese pupils there.
Elena caught pneumonia and sadly died during the
war while she was carrying out an order to entertain
Japanese troops with her dancing in South-East Asia.
Her sister was still teaching in Kamakura after the
war's end.

CHAPTER 11

Father's Sudden Death

✦

I WAS TWELVE when my father died of a heart attack in 1934 at the age of fifty-five. Among the people who came to the house, where he lay, to pay their respects was the mother superior of the St Maur Convent, who assured me that my father would go straight to Heaven. I was amazed by her words and deeply impressed, because at the convent school, at which I had just spent the preceding year as a regular student, I learned – although I was not Catholic – that when people die, everyone has first to go to Purgatory. My mother told me afterwards that Daddy had helped the nuns in some exceptional way, perhaps at the time of the earthquake, but his modesty was such that she never discovered what it was he had done for them. Likewise she and I remained ignorant of why gifted photographer Rikichi Matsuda was such a remarkably devoted general assistant of his. She had a vague idea that my father had saved Matsuda-san's life in some way. I recently donated to the Yokohama Archives of History a three-volume collection of Matsuda's photographs of every possible aspect of the earth-quake-levelled city.

Over a thousand attended the Buddhist ceremony at the Zemma Works, and his dear friend, Mayor Ariyoshi, later Governor of Kanagawa Prefecture, was one of the pall-bearers at the Christ Church ceremony on The Bluff. Flowers were sold out everywhere, for it was also the funeral of Admiral Togo of Russo-Japanese War fame, whom Frank admired.

Overworked and overstressed for many years, Frank Britton had longed for a holiday in England with his family, but had never been able to afford the time. His only relaxations were his cello, his study of astronomy, his collection of woodblock prints of old Yokohama, and the very few week-ends he managed to spend in Hayama – where he flatly refused to install a telephone! I often wonder what he would think today to see almost everyone, adults and children alike, talking on their mobiles and i-phones the whole time, even when walking down the street!

Frank Britton was liked and highly respected by not only the foreign residents, but also the Japanese leaders of the community. Mayor Chuichiro Ariyoshi became one of his best friends, and, after the earthquake, appointed Frank as Honorary Adviser to the City. Frank's major contribution to the City of Yokohama was a state-of-the-art refuse destructor, the finest, it was said, in the whole Far East. He travelled to England and throughout America in 1925 making a thorough study before designing what would be most effective and suitable for Yokohama. Completed in 1929 his incinerator was capable of burning 91,000 tons of rubbish per year, while at the same time contributing 12,500 kilowatts of electrical power to the city. Its design would still be called progressive today. It was moved to Hodogaya in 1942.

While in America, Frank was impressed by the ingenuity of design of the cement bags made by the Bates Valve Bag Corporation of Chicago, and he introduced production of these bags into Japan, setting up a factory adjacent to the Zemma Works. He appointed Dennis Kildoyle, the son of his early employer, as manager. Soichiro Asano of the Asano Cement Company became one of its principal shareholders.

Frank Britton was Vice-President of the Yokohama Rotary Club and truly embodied its motto: 'Service Above Self'. He was a man of wisdom, justice, infinite kindness and the soul of integrity and honour. In their *One Hundred Years of Hitachi Boilers*, Koichi Arai and Keitaro Tachibana wrote:

Britton was an important bridge between our nations, and with his early death Japan lost a true
friend who in his quiet way exerted enormous influence and forged a deep bond in Anglo-Japanese
friendship.

A fortnight after his death my mother and I were
called to the Yokohama City Hall, where, according
to the *Japan Advertiser* of 17 June:

> The Governor of Kanagawa Prefecture, Mr. S.
> Yokoyama, presented Mrs. Britton with a silver
> engraved cup and an illuminated scroll on Friday
> afternoon. The text of the scroll contains an
> expression of the appreciation for the contribution
> which the late Mr. Britton made during the 30 years
> he lived in Japan to promoting friendship between
> Japan and England, for his social work amongst the
> Japanese people and for the part he played in the
> progress of the engineering trade in this country.
> The scroll also states that it was largely through
> his efforts that the sanitary equipment of the city
> of Yokohama was improved, and concludes with
> the statement that this expression of appreciation
> is given in accordance with the promulgation
> issued at the time when the present Emperor was
> enthroned.

There was a representative of Emperor Hirohito
present, and I remember how tremendously thrilled
I was at the unexpected message he conveyed to me
from His Majesty, thanking me for having recently

come along the beach to the sea gate of the Hayama Imperial Villa with a bucket containing a specimen of the highly colourful sea-slug of the family *nudibranchia*, with its frills and decorative appendages. We had never seen one before, and I remember my mother suggesting I take it over to the palace and give it to one of the guards for the marine zoologist Emperor, who happened to be in residence. None of us had ever met His Majesty, although my parents were among those invited to his enthronement. The imperial *saké* cups that they received are still displayed in my dining-room beside a photograph of the present Emperor and family.

CHAPTER 12

England

✦

MY MOTHER AND I left Yokohama the following year
on the *Tatsuta Maru*, bound for Honolulu, where we
spent a week at the Halekulani Hotel on Waikiki
Beach. I shall never forget the fragrant lei and the
delicious cup of pineapple juice we were each handed
as we disembarked. It was my very first taste of pineapple! Mother looked up old family friends among
the early American missionaries, while I had some
lessons on my beloved ukulele that Aunt Dorothy had
bought in Hawaii on her way to Japan. My father had
worked out a few chords for me, and I already knew

one Hawaiian song a Japanese Hayama neighbour had taught me.

We were bound for England, via the USA to visit Mother's relatives in Oregon and California. Her unmarried cousin Isabella in Portland tried very hard to persuade us to settle there with her. Her mother, Mummy's favourite aunt, had just died, leaving a beautiful house and garden at the head of King Street. I went to Miss Catlin's School for several months while Mother thought it over, but she was determined to carry out Daddy's wish that I should go to an English boarding school. After a brief stop in San Francisco, we spent a few more months in America, down in Beverly Hills, where Mother's best friend Alice Baker Richards and her husband, now retired, lived. In a fine school there I fell in love with the works of Joseph Conrad and Thomas Hardy and they even had a harp teacher at the school, so I had a few harp lessons before finally setting off across the Atlantic Ocean, bound for my father's country for the very first time. On the ship we made lifelong friends from Bermuda. 'Where's Bermuda?' we had asked each other after lifeboat drill, where we had just met them! We found we had adjoining cabins, and like us, Doris Butterfield was taking her daughter Elizabeth to boarding school – the famous girls' school at Cheltenham.

Claremont in Surrey was a beautiful school in an old, historic building, but I was not very happy. Elizabeth Butterfield was not happy at Cheltenham, either, and ran away. I stuck it out, but I worried about my mother being lonely in a residential hotel, knowing hardly anyone in England. The only relatives we knew about were the Rendells. My father's first cousin Anna Bannister, whose parents had brought him up after his mother died, had married a Baptist preacher, and with their two daughters, Isabel and Joan, were living in Sydenham, in south-east London, in Anna Bannister's parents' house – the house where my father had spent his youth. My mother was over-joyed at finally meeting cousin Anna after having corresponded with her for so many years, ever since marrying Frank.

Anna, on her part, was sad that she could not have received Alice in proper style, in the Bannister's ancestral country seat, Corsham Court, near Bath, which should have been her father Alfred Bannister's, but for the skulduggery of a lawyer 'friend'. At Corsham, my mother could have moved in with Frank's cousins, and would have enjoyed the beau-tiful mansion with its garden where peacocks roamed, and would not have been lonely. Corsham had been the home of Anna's great, great uncle Captain Samuel Wallis, R.N. (1728–1795) who discovered Tahiti, and Wallis Island, which was named after him. His wife was a Bannister, but they had no children, and so it had been difficult to prove the relationship. The only registry of marriages in those days was at a church, and in the Bannister's case, the relevant page had been torn out.

I missed Japan so much. My happiest times at Cla-remont were some free periods in which I continued my study of written Japanese. I had the primary school textbook with me, the *shogaku kokugo tokuhon*, and was going through it methodically. How I loved those stolen periods. They took me back to my beloved Japan, for which I was dreadfully homesick. There was even a drawing of kites flying over the sea, singing *pii-hyara, pii-hyara, pii-hyarara!* Which vividly reminded me of my beloved Hayama. I taught myself the *hiragana* syllabary and was hard at work memorizing *kanji*, when one day a mistress came over and asked:

'And what are you doing?'
'I'm studying Japanese,' I explained.
'That's not on the curriculum of this school,' she said crossly. 'If you've got any spare time you should be spending it on your Latin.'

Being half American, I became friendly with a girl from the United States. It was just at the time that Edward, the Prince of Wales, had fallen in love with Mrs Simpson, and my friend had been sent lots of newspapers from the United States giving all the racy details which were absent from the British press, and we used to crawl under her bed to read them, frightened of being discovered. And then later on when the affair reached its peak and the Prince, who had become King Edward VIII, announced that he could not face going on being the monarch without the help of the woman he loved. Our Headmistress gathered all of the students together, on both the chairs and carpeted floor of the drawing-room, to listen to his abdication speech on the radio. It was 11 December 1936.

My mother and I had no home in England, a war seemed to be looming, so after two years we decided to move to Boston, where my mother had some very dear friends from her Japan days. Mrs Poole had come over to London for the Coronation of King George VI (12 May 1937), and persuaded us. I graduated from Miss May's, a very nice private Boston high school, aged sixteen – with a prize, would you believe it, in chemistry! The prize was a copy of Madame Curie's autobiography, for they were sure I would be following in her footsteps, but it was only the fascinating scientific nomenclature that had me in thrall! The school was opposite MIT (the Massachusetts Institute of Technology) on the banks of the Charles, which I used to spend time gazing at, and my poem *Mist on the Charles River* was published in the *Christian Science Monitor*, my very first published work, followed by a couple of nostalgic essays about Hayama.

CHAPTER 13

Bermuda

✦

BERMUDA WAS ONLY a day and two nights away from Boston by ship, and the Butterfields invited us for Christmas, and then the following year (1938) for Easter. So after graduation, when I was found to be suffering from eye strain, my eye doctor advised a bookless year for me, with plenty of outdoor life, before going on to Harvard's Radcliffe College, whose entrance examination I had passed. So we decided to spend that year in Bermuda – a stay that became extended because of the start of the Second World War.

I loved the outstandingly blue sky and sea of Bermuda, and still think of it as my second home. It had been an uninhabited island in the middle of the Atlantic Ocean, covered with palmettos and small cedars, until a Spanish pilot called Juan de Bermudez came across it by chance in 1505 as he was searching for a trade wind for home. The first record of its discovery appeared on a sea chart of the Western Atlantic in 1511. It was not settled until 1609, when the British *Sea Venture* ended up on its rocks instead of Jamestown, Virginia.

We rented three different houses a few doors away from the Butterfields on Pitt's Bay off Hamilton Harbour. Two of them were in the typical Bermuda style, white or painted in pastel colours and made of coral limestone dug from beneath to become the tank for the rain water caught on the white stepped roofs. In those days, no personal motorcars were allowed in Bermuda, and the only modes of transport were a few horse-drawn carriages and lots of bicycles.

I had never been in a sailing boat before, and was thrilled when a Bermudian girl I met called Ilys Darrell invited me to go for a sail with her in her twelve-foot dinghy. I was fascinated as I watched her pull up the mainsail, and at the same time I tried similarly pulling up the jib. It worked, and Ilys said: 'Ah, I see you are familiar with boats.' I kept quiet, and she soon offered me the tiller as we sped through the calm waters of beautiful Hamilton Harbour. This time I did not do quite so well, but it was only a wee bit of water that I took in over the side as we leaned over in the rather stiff breeze. Before too long I sensibly handed her back the tiller to complete our truly delightful, and for me my very first exciting, sailing trip.

I was well and truly hooked. I had noticed that a nice 'coloured man' (as they called blacks then) who looked after some of the yachts in Pitt's Bay had a small sailing boat of his own, and so I rented it, and invited my best friend Elizabeth Butterfield to come for a sail. They had a fairly large sailing boat themselves moored in the bay, which belonged to her brother, who had moved to Canada with his Canadian wife. But Elizabeth had never learned to sail, and accepted my invitation. Mother made sandwiches for us to eat on one of the little islands, and we cheerily set off. I sailed straight out of Pitt's Bay towards the opposite side of the harbour, speeding along in the good breeze and taking in no water, but as we quickly neared the land on the Paget side I suddenly realized I did not know how to turn around! Seeing my desperation, Elizabeth racked her brains and said 'I've heard my brother say something about going into the wind, whatever that means.' I tried it and it worked – so we neither capsized nor were hit by the boom – but I was terrified, and sailed straight back to Pitt's Bay, moored the boat, and we ate our sandwiches on the Butterfield's lovely lawn!

There were no native people in Bermuda when it was settled by the shipload of English men and women who were shipwrecked there in 1609. But much later they were joined by Portuguese and Africans, to help with various sorts of labour including house building.

One of the three houses my mother rented was quite large so we had a black lady to help us with cooking and cleaning. She was a truly delightful person, a schoolteacher, highly educated, and my mother greatly enjoyed their conversations together, and used to marvel how she ceased to seem black when they talked together. It bore out my childhood discovery that it is the way you sound that determines how you seem to look! And strangely enough, it was only yesterday that I read in an English magazine about a new wave of black Britons with beautiful English accents whose careers have flourished in the USA. Said British actor and playwright Kwame Kwei-Armah to Tim Adams in *The Observer*:

> All the stereotypes that used to attach to the Jewish community here, of culture and education and learning, have suddenly been attached to black Brits. We are given extra respect. You feel it when you start to speak. You have currency.'

The next day, after my attempted sail, I went to the Library and took out a lot of books about sailing, whereupon Ilys suggested I enter the twelve-foot dinghy races for under eighteens, for which she was no longer eligible, while I was still only seventeen. She lent me her dinghy, Number 5, and I still have the newspaper clipping about my first race. It ends with the words: 'Miss Button, sailing No. 5, came in last.' Being called Miss Button in addition to being last was doubly humiliating! Thanks to Ilys, I raced for two years in that splendid little boat, and once managed to come in third!

An amazing coincidence was finding that the Reverend Eustace Strong, the vicar of Hamilton's St John's church, and cousin of philosopher Lord Bertrand Russell, was the man who had christened me in Yokohama – the last baby to be christened before Christ Church on the Bluff was demolished in the Great Kanto Earthquake. He took me under his wing, and having no children, used to like to act *in loco parentis* to me. He was married to an American lady he had known in Yokohama who had lost her husband and children in the Great Earthquake. He fell in love with her in Hayama, he told us, while riding with a few of his parishioners, one holiday, in one of those little horse-drawn 'buses' we used to have there in those days. He had been tremendously impressed by her stoicism when the carriage hit a pothole and that lady's head was thrown against a hard partition. I joined his choir, and learned to love church music, and the way it emphasizes so effectively the imperative, essential, and challenging words of Jesus and Saint Paul, both of whom I passionately revere.

Having given up the violin, I was continuing with piano and when the British Censorship Headquarters took over the Princess Hotel, also on Pitt's Bay, which was owned by a relative of the Butterfields, I was thrilled when they asked us to give its Bechstein grand piano a home for the duration of the war! I was recruited by the Censorship Department as the only person in Bermuda who could read letters in

Japanese. Fortunately there were hardly any, for one postcard could take me a week even though I had a Rose-Innes, the most advanced kanji dictionary of those days, but not nearly comprehensive enough. When there was nothing in Japanese I was kept busy censoring letters in French. Paper must have been scarce in wartime France, for many people wrote in several directions, over what was already there, on the same page, which made letters difficult to read.

It was then that I discovered the difference between letters in French, and 'French letters' – British slang for condoms! Near us down the road from Pitt's Bay was a charming little guesthouse in which an English lady was spending the war years. She became quite a friend of my mother's, and every time we met she would tell us how many 'French letters' she had seen floating about on the water surrounding the guesthouse that morning. There could not have been much of a sewage system in those days! She used to see them when she was fishing for tiny bream in the bay from the guesthouse garden. I had always found it hard to believe they had so many guests from France, tourists being scarce during wartime! She also tried to persuade *us* to fish for bream too. Food was scarce, since Bermuda had always imported everything, being only a tourist destination. We tried fishing. But we hated taking the fish off the hook, and could not bear to have to kill it, so we gave up.

My mother helped organize and run a club for sailors, where I helped, too, in the evenings as waitress and dancing partner. There, my hobby of collecting folksongs in different languages got a tremendous boost when young men from all over the Commonwealth en route to England to join up came via Bermuda and I learned from them Maori songs of New Zealand, Afrikaans songs, and songs of various African tribes, to add to the songs of Hawaii and Japan that I already sang with my tenor ukulele at charity gatherings, calling myself 'Isabella with her small guitar'. Isabella is actually my first name. According to my mother, Belleville, New Jersey, got its name from all the Isabellas in the Scottish family of Duncans who settled there, one of whom married my maternal grandfather Dr Frederick Hiller Jr MD, the son of the former Prussian count, so Isabella was one of my mother's names, too.

Besides helping with the club, my mother organized regular visits to the Naval Hospital. It was at the other end of the island, whither our small group of volunteer women and girls were taken in a motor launch, carrying little bags of fruit and sweets for the patients. Having to make cheerful, encouraging conversation to strangers was a useful training for a shy teenager, but I wondered for years what my mother meant when she worried about one of the chaps making 'sheep's eyes' at me – apparently, shy amorous glances! Besides learning that funny American term, I also acquired a lifelong love of apples. My mother used to order crates of extremely succulent ones from Canada for those boys, and I used to pinch one each morning from her crate so I could eat an apple during the tea break, sitting alone on the sea wall of the Princess Hotel, communing with nature. I continue that habit I learned then, and now every evening, after supper, I eat a sliced-up apple in bed, while relaxing and reading the paper.

Everyone in Bermuda was doing some sort of war work. I tried to persuade Elizabeth to join us at the sailor's club, reminding her that even Oxford and Cambridge boys were sailors then since it was wartime, but she refused, saying she just did not like the uniform sailors wore! As far as I know there was no club for officers, but I think she had an officer boyfriend. If any of my sailor friends got serious, I told them I was in love with a place called Hayama. For it was true. At that time I really was not sure whether I could ever fall in love with a person!

I had always subscribed to *Punch*, a magazine I loved because its humour never failed to cheer me up if I was depressed, and during the war it was not only doubly helpful in that way, but kept me in touch with what was going on in England. I even cut out and kept the drawings I liked best. Elizabeth's mother did not join my mother in running the sailor's club, because she became busy in another organization concerned with looking after rescued victims of torpedoed merchant ships. So I was quite excited when I heard that Mrs Butterfield had one of the *Punch* artists staying with her who had just been rescued from a torpedoed ship on which he had been the radio operator. I asked her if she could bring Norman Mansbridge over one day for tea.

Norman and I got along like a house on fire. We liked all the same things, and I loved hearing about his description of sitting on *Punch*'s famous Round Table, where they commented on one another's drawings for that week. He loved music, too, and we used to sing madrigals in two parts that we both knew by heart, while treading water in Pitt's Bay! We were constant companions during the few weeks of our truly magical relationship. Norman said he had never felt so close to anyone before without physical contact. Our relationship was a perfect example of words quoted by Nietsche in his *Beyond Good and Evil* that had always impressed me deeply: *Dans le véritable amour c'est l'âme qui envelope le corps.* (In true love, it is the soul that envelops the body.) That made a lot of sense to me. The body *inside* the soul, rather than the other way around. In other words, sex should come after an orgasm of the mind and spirit. In an interview I once came across, Marilyn Monroe put it like this:

> The most unsatisfactory men are those who pride themselves on their virility and regard sex as if it were some form of athletics at which you win cups. It is a woman's spirit and mood a man has to stimulate in order to make sex interesting. The real lover is the man who can thrill you by just touching your head or smiling into your eyes – or just by staring into space.

My remarkable friendship with Norman took place almost at the end of our time in Bermuda – the few weeks after I had resigned from the Censorship Office. When our flight was delayed for about a week, I remember he said he felt as if he had been given a priceless gift. Oh, so did I! But alas, there was no future in it, since he was already married.

I had my last swim in Pitt's Bay the morning my mother and I finally left Bermuda by seaplane – a Trans-Atlantic Lisbon Clipper – on 15 August 1942. I wrote a poem in the aircraft:

At dawn the dim stars whispered to my soul
    Fly not away!
The dark water as I stirred alight
The sea's bright phosphorescent milky way
Murmured in dying bubbles round my face
    Fly not away!

The sunlight with a warm and carefree voice cried
    Fly not away!
The sunlight splashing spray into my face
Playful and unconsoling as the launch
Fast left behind the sad familiar land cried
    Fly not away!

But the soft clouds said come, unloose the trammels
    Of the earth, and fly
With love's new pinions you have found on earth;
Their strength will bear you. The regret will fade
    As the land, away.

And Norman sent me a poem *he* had written:

> So my heart does not belong to the grey deep-sea
>   ships?
> Yet it was they
> Who brought me out of the dark stifling cities
> To sunny harbours, away.
>
> O let me fly
> Forever from the caged urban mind
> Into the sun, with you!

In those days of the seaplane, the airport was an island in Hamilton Harbour, and I remember Mother and I waited for the departure sitting at a small table on the grassy lawn, sipping lemonade. There was a surprisingly long wait, but I did not mind at all, as one never got tired of the uncluttered beauty of the Bermuda landscape – the remarkable blue of the bay and the sky and the dark green of the cedar trees that used to cover all the islands.

They gave us nibbles as well to help pass the time, and although I was in a sort of reverie, thinking about Norman, people were complaining of the hold-up. And little did I know that I was the cause! Many years later, my mother and I paid a short visit to Bermuda and looked up a couple we had known very well. The Gilmores. She was an English pianist, and he was an American who had been brought up in Italy, and

82

spoke perfect Italian, and worked in the Censorship Office, as I had. 'I'm dying to ask you something,' he said. 'What on earth were those peculiar papers you had in your suitcase the day you left Bermuda in the seaplane?' I had no idea what he could be referring to. He said that besides censoring letters in Italian, he helped as Interpreter in other situations, and that was why he was at the airport. He explained that as I no doubt knew, passengers' baggage had to be checked since it was wartime, and they had found a strange document in my suitcase written by hand, full of the following sort of information: 'Page 1, *The Hoard*. Page 15, *Ring*. Page 23, *Sword*, Page 26, *Servitude*, etc.' He said they spent ages trying to work it out, and had even called in the special code-breakers. And then in desperation someone had said to him, 'I think you know Dorothy Britton. What do you make of this?' So he told them I was a musician, and maybe it had something to do with music. So finally they put it back in my suitcase and let the seaplane take off. I suppose they had thought I might be a spy, since I had lived in Japan and was leaving at the height of the war.

'Yes, you were right. It was musical.' I said to Mr Gilmore, and told him the story. It was a long story. When America entered the war, American sailors started coming to our sailor's club, and one of them was a singer with a beautiful tenor voice and we invited him to our house so he could sing while I or my mother accompanied him on our Bechstein grand. He was delighted, of course, but even more so when he discovered a copy of the piano score, with words, of Wagner's opera *Siegfried* on my piano. He asked if he could borrow it for the short time that his ship was in Bermuda, because it contained the aria he was planning to sing when he tried out for the Metropolitan Opera when he got home after the end of the war.

While I was at The May School in Boston, I became a great Wagner fan after seeing a performance of his opera *Siegfried* and learning about Wagner's celebrated use of leitmotifs – the recurrent themes associated with a particular character, idea or situation – and in New York before embarking for Bermuda, to stay, as we thought, only for a year, I had bought Gustav Kobbé's book entitled *Wagner's Music Dramas Analyzed,* and the piano score, with words, of *Siegfried,* in which I underlined all the leitmotifs in red.

When the American tenor came back with my *Siegfried* score, he said, 'See what I've done?' and showed me the result of how he had gone through it and made a list for me of the pages and names of the leitmotifs. He begged me to sell him the score, saying, 'Since you are leaving Bermuda so soon, all you need do is buy another copy of the piano score in New York at the same store where you bought this one, and simply underline the leitmotifs again.' He had taken so much trouble I did not have the heart to say no, so I gave him the score, refusing to take any money for it. But I am afraid I never got around to buying another copy of *Siegfried*. I am glad I let him have mine, and I hope it gave him some happiness to work on that aria, for sadly, he did not survive the war to try out for the Metropolitan.

CHAPTER 14

Mills College, 1943–1945

✦

IT WAS IN Bermuda that I began composing music. At the sailor's club we discovered a young English naval radio operator seated at the club's old upright piano who was a brilliant pianist and my mother invited him to come and use our Bechstein grand. Raymond Leonard was also a composer, and his works in the style of Prokofiev and Rachmaninoff inspired me to try composing too. When my pianist aunt Opal Hiller in California heard that I was composing music, she insisted I come to Mills College and study with the famous French composer Darius Milhaud, who was

Jewish and had recently arrived there as a refugee from the Nazis. I entered Mills in 1943, but to my great disappointment, the director of the music department informed me that I could not study with the famous French composer until I was a senior. I would have to wait three years! I was in the depths of despair.

And then a wonderful coincidence saved the day. I struck up a friendship with the only other English girl there. She had gone to school in France, and when she heard I spoke French, she said 'You must meet Madame Milhaud', and took me to their house on the campus and we found her in the kitchen. Madame Milhaud was delighted to meet someone else she could converse with, and asked me what I was going to study, and when I said music, she said, 'Oh, then you will be studying with my husband.' I told her I wanted so very much to do so, but they would not let me. She said, 'Oh, that will never do', and took me in to meet the great man. He was not well and was in bed. He asked me to show him my compositions, so I rushed up the hill to my residence hall to get them and left them with him. Next day I had a phone call from the Director. 'Mr Milhaud says you have more talent than most of his seniors and he wants you in his class.' I was in seventh heaven. It was all because I spoke French. It is truly amazing how one thing leads to another!

And it was also a proof of how important it is to learn foreign languages. I was able to return Milhaud's faith in me by winning a prize that first year for my song – a setting of Matthew Arnold's *Dover Beach*.

And while I was working on my music for these words:

> Only, from the long line of spray
> Where the sea meets the moon-blanch'd land,
> Listen! you hear the grating roar
> Of pebbles which the waves draw back, and fling,
> At their return, up the high strand,
> Begin, and cease, and then again begin....

Striving to capture that wave sound in music, picturing in my mind those waves I loved, imagining their sound as they broke upon the sand, I remember how homesick I became for our seaside house in Hayama.

It was fascinating studying with Milhaud. He had a great sense of humour. I used a volume of Bach's *Chorales* to write notes on because of its hard cover, and one day as I arrived for our lesson, he said, 'Here comes Dorothy, always with her Bach, to give an air of seriousness!' Once he told us that a San Francisco matron had asked him if it was true that his wife was his first cousin, and he had replied, 'Yes, and we have a son, and he has three legs, but we love him!' Their young son was a budding artist, and I have often wondered if he did well. When there was an exhibition by a Chinese traditional painter I remember he dismissed it as 'Trop mécanique'. After learning that I had come from Japan, Milhaud asked me if I knew Beaté Sirota who was a student at Mills, and whose Russian-Jewish pianist father taught at the Tokyo Imperial Conservatory.

I said I knew of her, but we had not met, since she lived in Tokyo and I lived in Yokohama. So he asked me if I would speak in Japanese with her on the phone, as he wanted to hear what that language sounded like. He got her on the telephone and we had a nice chat, and Milhaud was delighted. 'It sounds like ti-ti-ko-ko ti-ti-ko-ko!' he said. As a musician, he had been conscious immediately of the duple rhythm of Japanese! Beaté had already graduated and was just on the point of leaving Mills, so there was no opportunity for us to meet then, but I met her several times later, both in New York and in Japan. She became famous during the Occupation under General MacArthur, because she was the only woman on the panel drafting Japan's post-war constitution, and in it she managed to secure Japanese women's rights. She authored a memoir entitled *The Only Woman in the Room*.

My friends at Mills were international – British, Chinese and Yugoslav, as well as their very first black student, the niece of the president of Haiti, a charming girl who only spoke French! When my Aunt told friends with daughters at Mills that she hoped they were befriending me, she discovered some had said 'We would, but she goes around with such a weird crowd!' My Chinese friend had the room next to mine, where I saw my very first panda. It was an enormous stuffed one. I was staggered! I had never even heard of them before. She taught me some Chinese songs, so I enjoyed sounding Chinese, too.

I only spent two years at Mills College, so I never would have studied with Milhaud – which was my whole point of going there – if it had not been for that miraculous coincidence of speaking French, for at the end of the war in Europe I left for London, expecting to be married! In Bermuda, during the war, the officers on one of the great many Royal Navy ships that called there, organized a dance at which a handsome young lieutenant and I danced together so beautifully that we fell in love. I invited him home for lunch next day at our lovely little house on Pitt's Bay, where we played chess, a game we both enjoyed, and I took him for a sail in the twelve-foot dinghy Ilys had lent me which I kept moored in front of our house. But we had not gone very far in our sail around beautiful Hamilton Harbour, before he noticed that the Blue Peter was flying from his ship, which indicated that it was about to leave, so I had to drop him as quickly as possible at the nearest pier. In the months following I wrote a poem.

> There's a feeling I thought was forgotten,
> A candle I fancied put out
> Mid the faces and conversation
> And the laughter round about.
>
> Can a firefly's light of a moment
> Tonight be remembered tomorrow
> When the sunshine blinding and strong
> Takes back the light that we borrow?
>
> But when the music is playing,
> Music that makes pulses beat,

I feel a desperate longing
Fill my aching heart and my feet

For what I thought was forgotten,
A dance that was never too long;
Love in a moment begotten
Without even a song.

Not long after that his ship was torpedoed by a
German submarine. He was rescued, and then he
joined HMS *Repulse*, which the Japanese Navy sank
near Singapore in December 1941, four days after
Pearl Harbor. Michael was saved, but remained for
the rest of the war at a British naval base in Sri Lanka.
All the time I was at Mills we wrote letters back
and forth, and we seemed to have a lot in common
– chess, and even music. When he wrote that he
was returning to England and hoped we could meet
in London as soon as possible, I was quite sure we
would decide to marry, and even took a wedding
dress my cousin Patsy lent me.

After crossing the USA by train, in the next suite
to Mr Heinz – who was very friendly and promised
to send us a parcel of his famous Seven Varieties – my
mother and I arrived in London from New York,
just after the end of European hostilities, in the first
ship that had not had to zig-zag in order to avoid
enemy submarines. It was the Cunard Liner *Queen
Mary*, and I remember how its thick wooden deck
railings were a mass of carvings of names and initials
of the American troops who had sailed to Europe in

her when America came into the war. The wood was covered in plastic, presumably to preserve that graffiti for history, just like the centuries-old names I had seen on slabs at Stonehenge. It is interesting how with time graffiti becomes precious art!

CHAPTER 15

London, 1945–1949

✦

IN LONDON, HOTELS seemed to be full, and we only managed to get a room at the Grosvenor House Hotel, which we could not afford to stay in for more than a day or two. I had kept in touch with Norman Mansbridge and rang him. He said his wife Edna was working at the Strand Palace Hotel, and he was sure she could get us in there. Edna turned out to be a very special person, lots of fun, and immensely kind, and the two of them and their children, became very dear life-long friends.

After a week or two at the Strand Palace, where Michael and I had our first meeting, Mother and I found a flat off the Kings Road in Fulham. It had just been beautifully renovated, and Mother hired a Bechstein grand for me to practise on. But sadly, my envisaged marriage failed to take place!

For when we met in London and started going to concerts together, we found we did not enjoy music in the same way. I was interested in hearing new music by Debussy and Ravel, Stravinsky, Rachmaninoff and such like, while Michael did not want to hear any music he had not heard before. (I have always wondered how he managed to hear his Beethovens and Mozarts the first time!) And invariably he fell asleep at concerts, saying he liked nice, familiar music that put him to sleep! Somehow we just did not hit it off.

So we broke up, and I got a job in the BBC Japanese Section, in charge of selecting and introducing the records for the musical interlude in their daily post-war radio programmes beamed to Japan. It was fun being able to speak Japanese again. There were three Japanese announcers. One was Aiko, a beautiful lady who was said to be the person who inspired the main character in Richard Mason's *The Wind Cannot Read*. One of the men, whose name was Yamamoto, came from Canada, and one day when he exultantly announced he had just become a British subject, I said, 'Now you are English, why don't you change your name to Hillfoot, since *yamamoto* means the foot of a hill?' He immediately replied, with a strong Japanese accent: *'Aw naw, I havu much betta: Mountbottom!'*

Wasn't that brilliant? About twenty years later, when Boy Bouchier and I were married and went to the consulate in the Japanese Embassy in Grosvenor Square for visas for him and his son to come to Japan with me, who should we find on the other side of the counter but Mr Mountbottom. When, just for fun, I introduced him as such, Boy, who knew Lord Mountbatten well, was naturally startled!

I enjoyed working at the BBC. At first, I did not think they would take me. The lady interviewing me for the job asked me if I was 'tidy-minded', and I did not know whether I was or not. But later, I joined the BBC chess club, and she was a member too, and then I think she was happy she had taken me on. There was a nice canteen at the BBC premises in Aldwych, and the four of us, the three Japanese and I, often had lunch together there. One day, I was late joining them, and the canteen was crowded. I had no trouble finding their table however, because all three Japanese, nodding their heads in 2/4 time as they talked, made them stand out a mile! They seemed to be saying 'yes, yes, that's so' with their heads the whole time.

During wartime, the staff at the BBC had been predominantly female, but with the war in the Far East having then ended too, men had started dribbling back home. A very interesting man, called George Hills, who was partly Spanish, joined us as a programme assistant. I used to question George about the Spanish Inquisition because I had begun composing an opera based upon it. One day George brought a colleague to lunch. They had both fought in the army in Malaysia, and they were going to draft a letter together to the war-crimes trials authorities praising a Japanese naval captain they had admired greatly, and who they felt should not be accused in any way. Because of my Japanese background George asked me to join them.

During lunch, George's friend, Colonel Hall, turned to me suddenly and asked if I had ever been in Bermuda, and was my first name Dorothy? It suddenly came back to me then that he must be Wilfrid Hall the man our Cable & Wireless Company friends had said was the nicest young man they knew, and thought he was just the one for me! Wilfrid, known during the war, and since then, as Ted, had gone to Bermuda as a private tutor, after which he joined a local publishing company. He was very good at tennis. Being eleven years older than I was, he had felt I was much too young for him. And I had not fallen for him. But just before war broke out a French ship visited Bermuda, and French speakers were invited to a party on board. Wilfrid was there, having graduated from the University of Lyons, and he and I got along very well in French at that party. Meeting me again in London, 'Ted' Hall tried to see me and do things together as much as possible. He told me that when he was introduced to me at the BBC, not yet remembering me, he had fallen in love with my smile! Eventually, he joined the Foreign and Commonwealth Office and was posted to the Gold Coast, now called Ghana, where he worked for ten years until they became independent. When leaving for Africa, he asked if he could join me in the BBC

canteen for a farewell lunch on his way to Waterloo
Station to board the boat-train for Southampton. He
was a man of few words. When we had finished
eating he put his hand on mine, saying, 'I think you
are tops,' and was gone. Afterwards, I received a
letter written on the ship saying, 'Regarding what
I said at lunch, I would like to take it to its logical
conclusion.' Was that a proposal? I wondered.

But I had fallen for my boss, the head of the Japanese
Section. He was a fascinating Englishman who was a
leading light in the British Judo world, and spoke and
read Japanese. I loved the snippets of *Tsurezure-gusa*
he would share with me from time to time as he sat
at his desk studying the fourteenth-century 'Essays in
Idleness' by Buddhist monk Kenko Yoshida. It was
years before Donald Keene's translation. I remember
particularly 'Sweeping away a hundred troubles with
one laugh'. I liked that line so much I copied it down.
Trevor Leggett was a brilliant chess player, too, and
we often played on his tiny set while having lunch. He
made his moves quickly and got on with his lunch and
invariably won, while I spent so much time deciding
on my moves that I ended up with nervous indigestion,
but I learned a lot. My father had begun teaching me
how to play when I was very young, and I remember a
friend of my mother's amazement when I said I would
never marry a man unless he played chess!

During a holiday in Geneva I challenged a French
guest at the hotel my mother and I were staying in
to a game of chess. He replied he would be happy to
teach me how to play. I had a hard time convincing

him I did know how. Next day, I overheard him describing our game to his friends in French, ending with 'and with typical English *sang-froid* she beat me!'

Trevor and I enjoyed many marvellously interesting conversations while strolling through parks on part of our separate ways home from the BBC after work. He seemed to enjoy my company, but kept saying he was never going to get married, and urged me to find myself a rich man, so that if it did not work I would at least have the money! I found the friendship so frustrating that I left the BBC. I did not know about homosexuality then!

CHAPTER 16

Innocence and Ignorance

✦

I WAS JUST over twenty-one, and knew nothing at
all about sex. I had never even been told about the
birds and the bees, although at some point in my early
teens I remember finding a booklet about sex among
my underwear, which Mother must have put there,
but the style of the writing was so unappealing, it put
me off reading it. Instead, I asked Mother to tell me
about those sort of things, but all she said was that one
day I would find out, and that it was very beautiful.
She obviously had learned what she knew from my
remarkably kind and aesthetic father.

My mother had been brought up to think that innocence was beautiful in a young woman. But I think she was wrong. To my mind, innocence differs little from ignorance, which is not good at all, and can even cause great distress. For instance, years ago I had asked my mother what a bedbug was. She had the misfortune to come across them in China, and almost shouted, 'Don't let that dreadful word ever pass your lips again! *You'll* never see one.' But alas I did see one, and if I had known what it was, a most stressful experience for us could have been avoided. When we rented that attractive, newly decorated furnished flat, as well as putting in a grand piano, I saw a bedbug on the very day we moved in. Entering my bedroom, I noticed a strange insect on the pillow. It looked exactly like an apple pip except that it had legs. We could have moved out straight away, had I known what it was and told my mother. But it was not until after weeks of putting up with a terrible itching of our wrists – which we thought must be caused by some lack in our diet due to us not being used to the rationing – that we discovered its cause. The seams of the wooden beds were crammed with bedbugs as a result of the beds having been stored in a warehouse during the war, where furniture from all kinds of neighbourhoods affected by the bombing had been stored together. We reported it to the Borough Council, who came and took the beds away to be thoroughly cleansed and the ghastly pest exterminated, but repeated Council de-bugging had little effect, and after countless nights of sleeping on the sofa and paired armchairs we had to go to the trouble of finding a different flat.

Another example of my innocent ignorance was when a man in Bermuda I barely knew invited me to go for a moonlight sail in his boat. 'How poetic,' I thought – and surprisingly, so did my mother, who evidently did not have any idea what his intentions might be. What made his invitation seem particularly romantic to me was that a little earlier, he had strolled past our house singing in a beautiful tenor voice the words from the movie *Rose Marie*, substituting my name for that of the heroine: '*O Do-ro-thy I love you, I'm always dreaming of you.*' What girl would not be thrilled, especially when he turned out to be one of the leading members of our church choir. But there was nothing poetic about that sail. It was all I could do to reject his advances without us capsizing!

I still exchange Christmas cards with a handsome, charming but intensely shy member of that same choir. Herbert was so correct, and asked the Reverend Strong to formally introduce us. His manners and his purity impressed me so much I wrote a poem to him:

Where is the sham I saw erstwhile
The great deception
The art removed from art
And the world where nothing was sincere?
Suddenly I can see only the stars
And I seem to see in them
The very purity of heaven
Because in your eyes I see Truth.

I think some of the nicest young men are too shy to tell girls they love them. I feel very strongly that mothers and fathers should tell their sons and daughters all they can about men and women. I think parents should try and be like friends to their children, not like parents lecturing them, for children listen to their friends. And friends very often give wrong information. The only sex information I ever had from a friend was when her elder sister could not swim with us because she had just started menstruating. Sitting on the sand with me my friend said, 'Eleanor can't swim today because she has been cut. If you want to have a baby when you grow up, you have to let them cut you and make you bleed.' What an awful decision to have to make, I thought.

After the bedbug problem we finally moved to Dolphin Square. We were told about it by an elderly lady who was one of the first nursing trainees of Florence Nightingale, and spoke to us out of the blue in The National Gallery saying how much I resembled a lady in one of the old paintings! Dolphin Square, built in 1935, is a large square block of private apartments in Pimlico, near the Thames. It is only eight floors high and surrounds an estate containing a swimming pool, gymnasium, shops, and so forth. The writer and politician A.P. Herbert described it as 'a city of twelve hundred and fifty flats'! It is divided into 'houses' named after British admirals. We lived in Howard House. And very conveniently, there was a bus that ran straight from there to the Aldwych BBC building.

CHAPTER 17

Back in Japan – 1949

✦

As soon as the war was over, my mother became very eager to return to the land where she had been so extremely happy with my father. When we left Japan we sold our Yokohama house to the company. Unlike most people, my father preferred to live in his own house rather than a company house, and drive his own car. In his Will, he said he hoped the house could become a club for the staff. It was so for a number of years, but the lovely house, with its historic touches was finally torn down to make way for a parking lot!

We had let our Hayama beach house to the British ambassador Sir Robert Clive, after whose tenure various members of the embassy took it over. The last pre-war tenants were Vere Redman and his French wife, Madeleine. When he went back to the embassy after the war as Counsellor Information, he lost no time in requisitioning our house for the use of senior embassy staff. We were so glad he had, for otherwise we should probably have had to wait until the peace treaty was signed to get it back. On leave in London he called on us at Dolphin Square, and said: 'Dorothy, why not come back with me to Japan? I can offer you the job of librarian in the Information Section.' But since I would not have been able to take my mother with me, I decided to wait until we could both go back to Japan together. We finally obtained permission from SCAP (Supreme Commander Allied Powers) as 'commercial representatives to inspect property'!

We crossed America and travelled on the *President Cleveland*, chaperoning an elderly American general's widow whom my mother had known at the US army post in the Philippines when visiting cousins there as a young girl, and whose family had refused to let her make the trip alone. She was a whiz at Bridge, and kept busy and happy the whole time playing. My mother found several bilingual Japanese ladies she had known well in the old days, who were returning after having renewed pre-war US contacts in the education field. As for me, I blended in with a delegation of elites from various sectors of life in the Philippines,

returning from post-war refresher courses in the USA.
They befriended me as one of them after hearing me
sing Spanish folksongs I had learned at Mills from
some Venezuelan girls. My tenor ukulele was packed
in my luggage but I managed to borrow a guitar for
the concert by the passengers.

'Miz TQ', a still scintillating former 'southern
belle', had been determined to visit Japan now that
her old friend Douglas MacArthur was there, who,
as it happened, had taken over from her husband,
General T.Q. Donaldson, as Commander in Chief,
Philippines. With a trunk full of new clothes for the
parties she envisaged, she was met in Yokohama by a
colonel who had been her husband's aide, and who
kindly offered to put us up, too, on our arrival on
20 August 1949. The Colonel and his wife lived in the
prefabricated officers' quarters that filled Yamashita
Park during the Occupation. The park had been constructed along the edge of Tokyo Bay just after the
Great Earthquake of 1923 with all the debris from
the destruction of the city of Yokohama. Prior to that
the area had been known as The Bund.

Vere Redman came down from Tokyo to see us
the very next day after our arrival, and offered me
the job of Publications Officer in the Information
Section of the British Embassy, which during the
Occupation was called the United Kingdom Liaison
Mission. I accepted without hesitation. Mrs TQ
also lost no time in making her call on the Supreme
Commander. She was driven up to Tokyo by the
Colonel's wife. Mrs MacArthur merely received her

briefly at eleven o'clock, without so much as a glass of
fruit juice for refreshment. No invitations of any sort
were forthcoming, and the General made no appear-
ance. She had at least expected to be invited to stay
for lunch.

> 'Where's Doug?' asked Mrs Donaldson. Can't I see
> Doug?'
> 'The General does not see anyone socially,' Mrs
> MacArthur replied. 'The General works very,
> very hard.'
> 'But I am *sure* he'll see *me*'

Mrs TQ had persisted, but to no avail.

The dear lady simply could not believe it. On
the verge of tears back in Yokohama she told us in
her southern drawl, 'Why, ah once danced all the
way across the Pacific with Doug!' She had never
expected an overly warm reception from the second
Mrs MacArthur, whom she scarcely knew, but Doug,
if only she could have seen Doug, she was certain all
would have been quite different.

At least she was pretty certain the Colonel and his
wife would throw a party or two for her. But very
soon the Colonel's wife took to her bed with the
DTs. It appeared they were both alcoholics, and had
few friends. My mother and I were Mrs Donaldson's
last hope. But when our house, that she knew we
had rented to the British ambassador when we left
before the war, turned out to be not a grand house
near the British Embassy compound in Tokyo as she

had apparently fondly imagined, but merely a little summer cottage in the country, poor Mrs TQ was utterly devastated. In fact she suffered a nervous break-down and had to be put in the Occupation hospital, and as soon as she recovered sufficiently, we had to arrange for her return to the United States with all the dresses she had brought for the imagined partying. It was very sad. But it was certainly not a time for parties. General MacArthur's dedication to his job was awe-inspiring. He did indeed work very, very hard; the lights in his office were on until all hours. Crowds gathered at the entrance to his headquarters to see him arrive and depart each day as if he were royalty. Whether a kind of hero-worship or mere curiosity, I am sure the Japanese were impressed by his sincerity – a highly regarded trait in Japan – and they lined the roads for miles, sadly watching him go when he was 'sacked' by President Truman part way through the Korean War.

The Colonel who had been General TQ's aide graciously said we could go on staying with them as long as was necessary, but since his wife was a severe alcoholic, and when he began making passes at me, I rang Vere Redman to ask how soon they would be able to let us have our house back so we could move in. When I told him why I was in rather a hurry, he understood and kindly made our quick return possible, with the kind cooperation of Colonel Figgess the Military Attaché, and Henry Hainworth the Head of Chancery, and their families, who, together with him and his wife, were sharing the use of our house.

During the Occupation, Baron Dan's house across the road from ours had been requisitioned for the Commanding Officer of Camp McGill, an American base in Takeyama, down Miura Peninsular from us, which had formerly housed Japanese Marines, and is now the Japanese Ground Self-Defence Force's Camp Takeyama. One day, Colonel Figgess got into conversation with a Japanese man on the beach who happened to be the Camp McGill Commanding Officer's chef, and Colonel Figgess asked him if he knew of anyone who could help in the Embassy house and be a caretaker. The chef, whose name was Kaneko, delightedly called his wife from the town where she had been evacuated during the war. She was a lovely woman and we were so happy to be able to take her over as our housekeeper when the Embassy gave us back our house. Mrs Kaneko had never worked for anyone before. Mr Kaneko was a marvellous cook, and after the Occupation ended Mother found him several good jobs in Tokyo with foreigners who did a lot of entertaining. When he finally retired, he asked if he could make lunch for us each day just to keep his hand in!

One of the first things my mother and I did on being back in Japan was to find Kin-san, my old nanny who had saved my life in the earthquake. Up until the war, I had written letters to her in katakana, and received a few back in return, but of course there was no contact during the war years. We discovered she was living with her nephew and his family in a thatch-roofed farmhouse among the rice fields in Totsuka, halfway between Hayama and Yokohama. It was fourteen years since we had left, and all those years – most of them wartime ones – of helping in the paddy fields had left her bent double with rheumatism and hardly able to walk. The hospital we put her in for treatment was depressing. It had been recommended by our old friend Mrs Okubo's eminent Japanese doctor, but it was grubby and bleak. No food was provided, and nursing was only what was strictly clinical. Patients were required to bring their own helper, who not only cooked their meals right beside their bed, but attended to all the patient's non-clinical needs as well. It provided constant companionship, of course, and twenty-four-hour care of a sort, so I suppose there was something to be said for the old-fashioned system. But it is hard to believe nowadays, when hospitals in Japan are so spick and span and 'state of the art'. We eventually arranged for her to live out her days at a pleasant care-providing spa.

I started work right away as Publications Officer in Vere Redman's Information Section at the British Embasssy, then called UKLIM. I was billeted at the Marunouchi Hotel. It was only a stone's throw from Tokyo Station, and was once said to be the sort of hotel where men stayed when they told their wives they were off to Osaka on business! Souvenirs from all over Japan are still conveniently sold in a centre nearby, although the rebuilt hotel is now on the international circuit. For some time it catered especially to Australians, who may possibly still be assured there of a good strong cup of tea. During the Occupation, the hotel was run by the Australian Army and served mainly as a Tokyo billet for the Commonwealth Forces of Occupation based down in Kure and Iwakuni in the southwest.

My room at the Marunouchi faced the railway line, and trains went by constantly jam-packed with 'salarymen', all in black trousers and white, short-sleeved shirts, with fans tucked into their belts against the stifling humid heat, for there was no air-conditioning. Only four years had passed since the end of the war, and everyone was working terribly hard. I was not the only one impressed by the 'let's get on with the reconstruction of our country' attitude. An American uncle of mine, my mother's favourite brother, inventor and aviation pioneer Stanley Hiller, came to Japan in 1950 to talk to General MacArthur about the use of helicopters in the Korean War. Uncle Stanley had developed one of the early models, which he called a Hillercopter. While in Tokyo, he was immensely intrigued by the charcoal-powered taxis, which had some sort of burner in the boot. I remember how nice and warm they used to keep one's back in the winter! My uncle returned the following year to try and buy one of those cleverly devised contraptions, but by then there was not a single one to be found anywhere, not even lying discarded in the corner of a garage. My uncle was astounded by the industry and speed with which they had not only been made redundant, but had already been recycled.

Commodities were still scarce, inflation was rife, and a black market flourished. I wondered why a store in Hayama whose sign read: *hanaya* (Flower Shop) contained only American packaged goods at inflated prices, and I realized post-war austerities were well and truly over when the shop started selling plants and flowers again as befitted its name. To make ends meet, our Japanese friends were living what they called a 'bamboo shoot existence', peeling off and selling layer after layer of family heirlooms, just the way one peeled off the outer skins of bamboo before boiling the delectable shoots. Many invested in knitting machinery and sold sweaters they made, and even former princesses who had once done wood-carving as an elegant pastime, carved objects for sale. And everyone made the best of things, and not a soul complained.

The Japanese were indeed working very hard. I was particularly amazed by the way nobody talked about the war. That was all people were talking about in England in 1945 when I arrived there from America just after VE Day, and I expected it would be the same in Japan. In fact, I was interested in hearing what they would have to say about the war. But everyone seemed far too busy looking towards the future to dwell on what was past. Perhaps the Japanese were so used to earthquakes, tsunami, typhoons and similar disasters that traditionally they avoided wasting time talking about such things. You just picked yourself up and got on with whatever had to be done. What our friends did say was that it was worth losing the war to get rid of the militarists. And a taxi driver told me what an immense relief it was to be able to call a monkey-wrench a *monkii* again. He told me that during the war English words were taboo, and it was so difficult to remember the complicated obligatory Japanese equivalents for parts of cars. One of the few Japanized words that *has* remained is *yakyu*, literally 'field ball'. It is so much more euphonious than *bee-suboru*, the unwieldy *katakana* Japanese pronunciation of 'baseball'.

My work as Publications Officer included book rights negotiations. Japanese wishing to translate a British work had to go through me, and I would bank the advances and the royalties. It was fun meeting the publishers when they came to collect the money. Young Peter Pitman of Pitman's Shorthand arrived during a holiday when the banks were closed, so I invited him down to Hayama, and his family became very good friends, and as a result, his daughter Joanna ended up studying Japanese at Cambridge under my friend Dr Carmen Blacker, and eventually became Japan correspondent for *The Times!*

Often publishers wanted to meet their Japanese counterparts, and while interpreting for them I discovered the importance of patience. Most Japanese, not being good linguists, were usually so slow in replying to questions that the Britishers often failed to get the information they hoped for. For instance, after an irritating long pause the English publisher would say, 'Well, do you think such and such?' to which the Japanese would just heave a sigh of relief and reply, 'Yes, yes. Quite so.'

Learning to be patiently silent served me in good stead at Japanese receptions. Having had it drilled into me for years that it was not done to stand around silently at parties, it was a relief to find it perfectly acceptable in Japan to wordlessly enjoy the canapés like the others. On the other hand, when there is a celebrity at the party, they tend to gang up around him or her, eager to have a word, and then do not know when or how to leave and give others a chance! The art of party conversation is quite new to the Japanese. Later, for several years, I taught English party conversation at a women's university.

CHAPTER 18

Love and Sex

✦

OCCUPIED JAPAN TURNED out to be a rush course for me in love and sex! Many were the single members of Commonwealth business, military and diplomatic staff I was domiciled with in that British Commonwealth billet. Almost the first evening I was there, the attractive New Zealand Representative greeted me on the stairs with the strange words, 'You strike me as every inch a woman!' inviting me for a cup of coffee in his suite. On learning I had never had a lover, 'It's nice' he said, and talked me into letting him give me an idea, gently, with his hand, what it was like. It did not thrill me at all, but we remained friends. He had a beautiful voice and I accompanied him once or twice on the hotel piano, but he was eager to find a girl to take skiing in the mountains, which was not my 'cup of tea', being a beach and sea person. But beautiful divorcée Marion Beverly (known as 'Bev'), who joined the Information Section as Vere Redman's shorthand typist at the same time I arrived, filled that bill perfectly, and she also became a very good friend of mine.

An Australian army major, who had come up to Tokyo from Kure, the British Commonwealth Occupation headquarters, to adjudicate a court-marshal, became seriously entranced with me, and actually proposed marriage, after expressing his feelings in a truly beautiful poem. But sadly I was completely put off by his obesity and insatiable appetite. Joining me for breakfast one morning, he ate everything on the copious menu and still wanted more. When I hinted he should go on a diet, he expressed great disappointment that I, the intellectual and aesthete who had appealed to him so greatly, could not see beyond the outer man. He was quite right, of course, to my shame.

Later, I met a very handsome, slim young army captain who arrived at the Marunouchi, and this time our love was mutual. But he was soon transferred to Hong Kong and bade me a fond farewell, saying how much he wished he could take me with him, but there was a reason why he could not. Giving me a beautiful pearl brooch to remember him by, he said he would write and tell me why. I, of course, imagined he must already have a wife. But when his letter came, he wrote that it was because he was half Indian! He gave no address. I dearly wished I could have told him that his being half Indian would have only made me even more eager to marry him, because to me all the peoples of the world are one. For I believe the words of Saint Paul: 'There is neither Greek, nor Jew, Barbarian, Scythian, bond nor free, and Christ is all in all.' Strangely, many, many years later, a friend of mine who lived in Japan had met him in a hotel in Scotland, and he had asked if my friend knew Dorothy Britton, with whom, he said, he had fallen deeply in love. But sadly, my friend had failed to get his name or address!

And then there was my boss, of all people. One day Mr Redman phoned from his house in the Embassy compound requesting me to come over to discuss something or other, and when I rang the bell he opened the door and furiously slammed it in my face. Utterly bewildered, I went back to the Chancery and told his Number Two, the Assistant Counsellor Information, who was in the office next to his, who replied, 'Oh, don't you know? He's in love with you.' It was all very confusing. The following day, I was sitting in my office unable to work, just feeling utterly dejected and downcast having been yelled at by my boss that I was a 'chicken-brained nincompoop'. And then a little while later a young woman who had just arrived in Japan came in from his office next door to mine saying that Mr Redman wanted her to meet me because he said I was brilliant and would tell her so much more about Japan! I told her what he had called me, and what a relief it was to hear she had been told I was the opposite! She was the Carmen Blacker mentioned above, who became one of my dearest friends. Carmen went on to get a doctorate at Tokyo's Keio University while writing a highly acclaimed book about its founder Fukuzawa Yukichi entitled *The Japanese Enlightenment*. Later, she became a noted lecturer on Japan and the Japanese language at Cambridge University.

Not long after all that, looking for something in a file, I came across a letter Vere Redman had written to a Foreign Office colleague describing his visit to my mother and me in Dolphin Square, saying: 'The daughter has turned into an intellectual and a beaut.'! It was very bracing, since I had always had an inferiority complex about my looks. When he got used to the fact that his apparent love for me was going to remain unrequited, he began to treat me better, and I eventually became a great admirer of Vere Redman, in particular for an extremely rare quality he possessed: that of being a marvellous listener to people's problems. All sorts of people with problems used to join the Redmans for breakfast, for no matter how busy he was, Vere would give one his full attention as if one's problem was the most important thing in the world. There was even one case where he went to the extent of perjuring himself to help out a friend who was in trouble.

Later, I was to learn about homosexuality when I fell in love with an actor. When 'majoring' in music at Mills I 'minored' in drama, and have taken part in many amateur dramatic performances, beginning with Molière's *L'Amour Medecin* directed by Madelaine Milhaud, the composer's wife, who had been an actress. So back in Japan I soon joined the Tokyo International Players. The TIP was the descendant of Tokyo's ADC (Amateur Dramatic Club) that I had heard so much about from my parents in the days when their friend Mrs de Haviland, mother of famous Hollywood star Olivia de Haviland, was a member. My mother was part of the ADC herself for a while when she substituted for the regular pianist who provided the background music for plays and silent films. When we were in California, Mother and I looked up Mrs de Haviland, whose second daughter Joan Fontaine was with her. I remember telling Joan I wanted to be an actress too, and she rather scornfully replied that every girl says that! Joan, who had taken her mother's second husband's surname, went on to be almost as famous as Olivia, but it said in her recent obituary that she and Olivia were sadly not on speaking terms.

Only three months after my arrival back in Japan, in December 1949, I played Monica, the young secretary in Noel Coward's *Present Laughter*, opposite Grant McIntyre, a very attractive Australian actor who had studied with Noel Coward before being called up in the army for wartime duty. I was much encouraged by poet Edmund Blunden's letter saying he 'enjoyed my study of Monica in every particular' and Diana Parnham Wyatt, who had been a star on the Australian stage until her marriage to a military man in the Occupation, who played Joanna, invited me to dinner with Grant, saying she was sure he had fallen in love with me. She wanted to encourage it, although, she said, he was a bit weak on sex, which she would try and do something about. But he held my hand in the taxi, and warmly hugged my shoulder, which gave me hope. But when I mentioned him during a conversation back in our hotel lounge, my New Zealand acquaintance said, 'He's a flair,' which seems to be the way they pronounce 'flower' in New Zealand. But I thought it just meant he was effeminate, and I have always rather liked a bit of womanly gentleness in men.

CHAPTER 19

Meeting 'Boy'

✦

MY MOTHER WAS jealous of my living in Tokyo, and asked if I could not get her into the Marunouchi Hotel. I managed to persuade the Australians who ran it to let her have a room there. She and I were having lunch together in the dining-room one day, when the jolly British Cable and Wireless Company representative, who lived there, came by our table with another gentleman who was a new arrival. 'May I introduce Air Vice-Marshal Bouchier?' he said. After commanding the British Commonwealth Air Forces of Occupation at war's end in Iwakuni until

1948, as well as acting as Commander-in-Chief for part of that time, the AVM had taken early retirement to represent the Confederation of British Industry (CBI) and was staying at the hotel.

My mother was awfully impressed, and said to me excitedly when they had gone, 'I've never met an Air Vice-Marshal before! Let's ask them both to Hayama for lunch on Sunday.' The Cable & Wireless man was a popular resident of the hotel, fond of horse racing, who used to organize betting on the annual Grand National held at Liverpool's Aintree race-course. The Air Vice-Marshal reminded me very nostalgically of my father and was fifty-four, the age at which my father had died. After lunch at our house by the sea, my mother took the two men for a leisurely stroll along the beach, while I sat on the steps and painted a water-colour of the scene. I had studied water-colour painting in Bermuda, and now that I was back in Japan, I was anxious to capture the Isshiki Beach scene that I had loved so much in my childhood days. The Air Vice-Marshal liked my painting enormously.

As Christmas approached, we heard there was to be a gala weekend party at Kawana, the ritzy resort hotel, with its two golf courses, on the Izu Peninsula, that the British Commonwealth Occupation Forces had commandeered for holidays. There seemed to be no places available for newcomers Bev and me, and Bev urged me to ask the AVM, whom I had just met, if he could use his influence to get us in. He kindly obliged, but when we got there we found he expected us to join his party, which included General Robertson, the

British Commonwealth Commander-in-Chief. For me, this was rather awkward, because I was expecting to spend my time with Grant, who was waiting for me and straight away asked me to dance, which I joyfully did. I was in seventh heaven until suddenly, in the middle of our first dance together, he said he did not feel well and had to leave the room. He did not return, so I was worried and wanted to see if he was all right, and found his room. There were three in each room for the men as well as the women, for that crowded Christmas occasion, and one of Grant's room-mates came to the door and got rid of me rather unkindly, assuring me Grant was perfectly all right.

On the way back to the ballroom I was buttonholed by a rather vulgar man who said he was Chief of the Australian Mission, and out of the blue asked would I care to be his mistress? He was either a divorcé or widower. 'All you'll have to do is look after the silver,' he said. What a strange evening, I thought. I later heard he was so extraordinarily straightforward and outspoken that he was known as the man who does not call a spade a spade, but calls it a bloody shovel! I was soon rescued by a call to join the C. in C. and AVM at a movie that was about to begin. Bev was already there.

Next morning, the Occupation's manager of the resort hotel, an Australian who was Grant's good friend, got in touch with me to say that Grant had been suddenly called back to Tokyo, and from thence, was ordered back to Australia. Seeing my distress the Manager invited me for coffee in an ante-room, where he played a record of my favourite Rachmaninoff piano concerto to try and calm my nerves and cheer me up. Later, the AVM asked me to join him for lunch, and afterwards invited me to go round the beautiful seaside golf course with him. He took along the pro, who gave me some free lessons, which was altogether very cheering indeed.

That night, my room-mate Bev, who, being a divorcee, knew all about men, explained to me that Grant was a homosexual, and though obviously fond of me, while dancing with me must have realized that marriage with a woman was not for him. My Occupation course in love and sex was now almost complete! I had learned about homosexuality, and soon after that I found out about trans-sexuality too. One day, when I came back to the Marunouchi Hotel for lunch, there was a fuss of some sort taking place at the bedroom opposite mine. The door was locked, and its owner, a girl who also worked in the Information Section with me, could not get in, and had called the staff. It turned out that a young Australian soldier had entered the hotel and locked himself into her room, and had been trying on all her clothes. When he was discovered, he burst into tears. It was sad. I went on to learn to know and like many homosexuals, and to wish so much that society was not so cruel to them.

Back in Tokyo, my mother, who needed a chauffeur, heard that someone at UKLIM was going back to England and wanted to sell their Austin, so she bought it for me, hoping I could soon learn to drive. Next day, the Accountant phoned me to say that my driving licence was in my pigeon-hole. 'But I don't know how to drive,' I said. He repeated what he had said and hung up. Back at the Marunouchi Hotel, when I joined my mother and the Cable & Wireless man and the AVM for a drink before supper, I mentioned this, whereupon the AVM offered to teach me.

He had, in fact already made some advances towards me. He had taken me to a movie that was being shown at the Imperial Hotel, and when we returned to our billet, he suggested I come up to his suite for a nightcap. There I was amazed to see a most beautiful small antique black lacquer bucket decorated in gold. He told me it had been sent to him by the dowager Countess Kikkawa to welcome him back to Japan. There is a photograph of it in his autobiography *Spitfires in Japan*.[1] When he was C-in-C British Commonwealth Air Forces of Occupation in Iwakuni, he had let her remain in part of the house belonging to Count Kikkawa, the feudal lord of Iwakuni, which had been requisitioned for the AVM. Next day I came back after work to find that fascinating antique lacquer bucket in my room filled with a huge mass of red roses. It was the first time I had ever received flowers from a man. I reciprocated by asking the maid to hang in

[1] *Spitfires in Japan*, Air Vice-Marshal Sir Cecil 'Boy' Bouchier, edited by Dorothy Britton, Global Oriental: Folkestone, 2005.

the Air Vice-Marshal's suite the water-colour I had painted in Hayama, which he had praised so highly. I had put it in a simple bamboo frame, and it was hanging in my room.

'Boy' Bouchier was enchanted, and soon gave me the driving lesson he promised. There was hardly any traffic in those days. At one point, we parked the car and strolled about, kissing right in the middle of the beautiful square in front of the Imperial Palace, where now traffic is many lanes strong. How strange it was to have learned how to drive while already in possession of a licence! Three years later, when the Peace Treaty was signed (1952), all I had to do was exchange it for a real one at the local police station.

Boy was called back into the Royal Air Force the following year, 1950, and returned to Tokyo to represent the Prime Minister Winston Churchill and the British Chiefs of Staff at MacArthur's headquarters during the Korean War. This time he was given a suite at the old Imperial Hotel, designed by Frank Lloyd Wright. It was the American Occupation billet for colonels and above. Very soon after he arrived back it was Valentine's Day, which is my birthday, and Boy came and fetched me for a birthday dinner with him there, although it was snowing quite hard. It was my very first meal at that famous hotel, and so when we sat down at our table I gazed around the dining room with great interest, and was chided severely by Boy. 'You should not look around. You should concentrate on the man you are with,' he said.

I am afraid my mother had failed to teach me that. When we had finished our dinner and it was time for me to leave, the snow was too deep for cars. Boy had to use his influence to obtain a jeep from SCAP headquarters. He told me that next day many female dinner guests were still there for breakfast! But I had not dared to stay overnight for fear it would upset my mother. We were heavily snowbound this year's Valentine's Day too, and the *Japan Times* reported it as the worst blizzard in sixty-four years. That is exactly, to the day, how long ago that birthday dinner with Boy was! It made me very nostalgic.

While he was billeted at the Imperial Hotel, Boy used to ring me almost every night to recite Shakespeare sonnets to me over the telephone. He also spent many weekends with us in Hayama, and I became deeply in love with him. He was twenty-six years older than I was, but he never seemed a day older, he was so young at heart and physically athletic. We walked for miles along the beaches, which he loved, and I taught him how to sail. We used to hire a small sailing boat that was moored off our beach in the summer. I also taught him chess. My mother was fond of him too, although it troubled her greatly that I was in love with a married man. 'He's so nice, Dorothy,' she used to say, 'but it's wrong, it's wrong. He's married.' Boy had told me right in the beginning that he had vowed never to leave his wife no matter how wonderful a woman he might encounter. I admired him greatly for that. He writes in his autobiography:

At the outset, I had told Dorothy I was married and that I loved my wife with all my heart, and because of this, we both vowed to keep our friendship a light and lovely thing, and not to fall in love – for we knew that it would only end in hurt for all of us. But as time went by, inevitably we fell in love with one another.

At the time we first knew each other I naturally asked Boy if he had any children, and he had replied in the negative. Then, finally, he told me about Derek. It had been such a tragedy for him that he could hardly bear to talk about him, so he usually just said 'no' when asked, until he knew people better. They had lived in a small flat five flights up over an ironmonger's store, and while he and his wife were away watching the annual inter-services RAF/Army rugby match, the maid had been carrying Derek and they fell on the steep stairs, leading to a severe convulsion for Derek which impaired the speech side of his brain.

When Boy had to return to England it was a very sad parting for both of us, and I could not stop crying for days. I had even suggested I marry his son Derek in order to be able to stay near Boy, but of course that was not possible. Boy writes in his memoir that during the long flight home he could not keep the tears from *his* eyes either. I did not think I would ever see him again, and it seemed to me just as if a spouse had died.

CHAPTER 20

Society in Japan

✦

MY EMBASSY BOSS, Vere Redman, the Counsellor Information, had been instrumental in starting up Tokyo's Japan-British Society after the war, and he persuaded me to join it soon after I became a member of his staff at the Embassy in 1949. But I found the gatherings at the Japan Industry Club terribly boring. None of the Japanese men brought their wives, and the food was awfully dull. The Council of the Society were unhappy about the small membership, as well as the fact that Japanese member's wives took so little interest in it.

1

Alice Hiller en route from San Francisco to Shanghai in 1920;
she stopped for three days in Yokohama and met Frank Britton

2

3

Frank Britton's house
in Yokohama c.1920
and (3) the same house
improved and enlarged
following his marriage in
Shanghai to Alice Hiller
in July 1920

Frank and Alice making music together during Alice's
pregnancy. Seated in armchair is Dorothy, Alice's younger sister

Dorothy Britton, not yet two, in the
family garden with her aunt Dorothy

6

The Great Kanto Earthquake 1923. A building similar to this crushed Dorothy Britton's aunt Dorothy and a friend

7

After the earthquake: Christ Church, Yokohama, where Dorothy Britton had been christened

8

Frank Britton's, office survived the earthquake as a result of his strengthening of the main structure

9

Kin-san – Dorothy Britton's nanny

10

Following the earthquake, having relocated Dorothy and Alice in Kyoto, Frank Britton (centre, first row seated) shares the family home with his colleague Tom Chisholm (end of row seated) and a contingent of military police seen here in the garden of the house

Dorothy with Wakako – daughter of Okubo Toshimichi – photographed with her tall elder sister and Mrs Okubo in the dark kimono. Both children were the same age and remained the closest of friends

Friends participating in Dorothy's Valentine's Day fancy dress party in the Britton house in Yokohama. Dorothy is front row, second from left

Dorothy aged c. six photographed among young pines at the new house in Hayama

14

Departing for England on the *Tatsuta Maru*, 1935,
following the death of Frank Britton the previous year

15

Frank Britton's cousin Anna Rendell seated next to
Dorothy, with the Rendell daughters Joan (left) and
Isabel standing. Standing centre back is Alice Britton

16

The Butterfield's sailing boat at Pitt's Bay, Bermuda

French composer Darius Milhaud with
whom Dorothy studied composition at Mills
College, California, in 1943

Dorothy photographed with the
niece of the President of Haiti
– the first black student at Mills
College

19

Dorothy singing folk songs with her ukulele at a garden fete. At the time she was working for the BBC

20

Dorothy eventually switched from the ukulele to playing the Irish harp

21

Dorothy and Alice Britton returned
to Japan in 1949, together with 'Mrs
"TQ"' (far right)

22

23

The British Embassy, Tokyo,
where Dorothy was Publications
Officer. Inset (23) Queen
Victoria's God-daughter Victoria
Drummond – at the time the
world's only female ship's engineer

At work on the Dorothy Britton Cantata with
librettist Elizabeth Baskerville McNaughton (left)

Dorothy interpreting Ikuma Dan's talk about Japanese music
for the Tokyo English Teachers Association, c. 1956

26

Ikuma Dan conducting the CBC Orchestra for
Dorothy Britton's Cantata in Japanese

27

The first performance of Dorothy Britton's
'Madame Beggar' took place in Nagoya in 1960

28

Cartoon featuring Dorothy teaching
English and singing British folk songs
on NHK's weekly programme for
Junior High Schools

29

Alice Britton (standing right) with
dowager Princess of Kitashirakawa
and daughter Princess Sawa
photographed with Dorothy
(seated) under the thatched roof
gate of their Hayama villa

30

Young elephants photographed on the deck of
the *Maori*

Charles Britton at his house on The Peak, Hong Kong

Charles Britton's yacht

33

Photograph of pelagic nudibranch *Glaucus* that floats among the sea's 'Blue Layer' creatures

34

Norah and Dorothy Britton eating fresh sea urchin on Ishigaki Island

35

Australian zoologist Isobel Bennett who joined Norah and Dorothy on Ishigaki Island

Local Rotary Club celebrates 2009 Rotary Centennial with a
statue of Basho at New Shirakawa railway station, including
Dorothy Britton's translation on plinth of Basho's words: 'It
was not until we finally reached the checkpoint, or barrier
at Shirakawa that we felt we were really on our way at last'.
Dorothy can be seen on the right speaking at the official
opening ceremony

The Bouchiers (from left): Derek, Dorothy and Boy
in front of the house designed by Frank Britton

38

Wilfrid 'Ted' Hall in the early days in
Bermuda when Dorothy first met him

39

1993. Ted Hall (far left) with Derek, Dorothy and Anne
Collier and friend in Connecticut. Anne's older brothers
appear as two little white-trousered soldiers in Plate 12!

Although the Japanese are really not very different from the British in many ways, certain customs and institutions are quite dissimilar. One of the most notable differences is that in Japan there is no 'society' as we know it. The lack of 'society' such as we know it in the West, makes for almost no snobbery or class distinction in Japan: if there are no parties there is no nonsense about who is invited to what parties and who is not. There is also no pretentiousness or ostentation.

Wives do not help their husbands entertain. They almost never accompany their husbands to parties, and at restaurants the feminine company is provided by the geisha, who sit by the table and join in the conversation, although they do not eat with the men. It is rather difficult for a Westerner to understand exactly what a geisha is because she has no counterpart in the Western world. In the West, the ordinary woman, besides being a daughter, wife or mother, like any Japanese daughter, wife or mother, plays much of the additional role of the Japanese geisha as well. In other words, one Western woman plays the part of two Japanese women. The geisha part is that side of the Western woman who mixes with the men at par-ties, flirts with them, dances with them, and amuses them with witty conversation as well as laughing at their jokes and being an intelligent listener. She takes a lot of trouble with her looks and her clothes, and is, in short, an accomplished and attractive companion who entertains so splendidly and is such a lot of fun at parties.

In Japan, when a man entertains at home, his wife helps serve the food, but usually does not sit down to eat with the men or even converse much with them. This is, of course, gradually changing but it will be a long time before ordinary Japanese women take an active part in society because they are not yet trained in this from youth as Western women are. Western girls as well as boys are trained from childhood in the art of making conversation with strangers, and in how to do their part in making a party a success, for boys and girls start going to parties early. But in Japan there are no parties such as we know them. Parties are usually business parties given by companies for their clients where business may be transacted, and they take place usually at restaurants with geisha in attendance. There are also many formal receptions, such as wedding receptions, and company anniversaries, and parties such as those given by broadcasting and recording companies for their artists and clients. But there are simply no parties just for the sake of getting together and having fun, and conversation has never been developed for its own merits. Japanese young people associate with their schoolfriends, with whom conversation comes easily, but they do not have to make conversation with strangers or with their elders. If visitors come to call on their parents the children are not expected to come in.

In 1959, Vere asked me and Kazuko Aso, the daughter of Prime Minister Yoshida, to join the Council of the Japan-British Society – which had never before had any female members. Kazuko, brought up in England, whose English was almost better than her Japanese, immediately livened up Council meetings with her sense of humour and pertinent comments on how to improve Anglo-Japanese relations, while I stuck to mundane things like food, suggesting, for instance, that they put chocolate sauce on their usual plain and dreary little scoop of vanilla ice-cream, which they invariably served for dessert. Accordingly, the fare at the next gathering was a considerable improvement. But at the following Council meeting Vere Redman said, 'Dorothy, we didn't put you two girls on the Council so that we could have chocolate sauce. We put you and Mrs Aso on it to think up activities for lady members. So please get on with it!' But the British men on the Council shook their heads, saying, 'It's no good. You'll never get Japanese wives to come to anything.'

So on 9 July 1959, Kazuko and I had tea at the Marunouchi Hotel to discuss what we should do. I told her how I had noticed at the Tokyo International Women's Club, where I had performed my programme of folksongs, that the English-speaking members tended to congregate in one part of the room and the Japanese speakers in another. There was nothing international about it, and I kept wondering how one could get members in a club like that to mix so that international friendships could be fostered – for that is what the world needs so badly.

And then I told Kazuko about the Nadeshiko Kai – a posh but very unusual new club my mother was a member of. She and a friend had been asked to join as their first foreign members. The *nadeshiko* is a pink, a demure little flower of the genus Dianthus which is thought to represent the ideal Japanese woman. The club had been started by a bilingual Japanese lady called Mrs Enomoto, who had spent many years in America, and taught English. It was made up of small groups, each consisting half of Japanese women and half of English speakers of various other nationalities, including many wives of ambassadors. Every month the groups did something interesting, and the make-up of the groups was changed each year. And moreover, there was no committee and no paperwork. Each month the groups would decide what to do the following month, so no notices had to be sent around. I thought what an ideal arrangement!

Kazuko was impressed, and we decided to start JBS women's activities along those lines. First of all, of course, I asked Mrs Enomoto, if she had any objection to our imitating her splendid society, and she very kindly encouraged us to do so. Perhaps she knew the English expression: 'imitation is the sincerest form of flattery'. A week later, Kazuko Aso invited to her home fourteen lady members of the Japan-British Society – seven British and seven Japanese – and we told them about our plan and asked them if they would care to volunteer to head, in Anglo-Japanese pairs, seven small groups of about twelve ladies each, half British and half Japanese.

The day Kazuko and I were having tea at the Marunouchi Hotel, the British Ambassador, Sir Oscar Morland, was out of the country at a conference,

I think in Thailand, and Alice, Lady Morland, was spending the weekend at Hayama with my mother. When I got home that evening, Lady Morland was delighted to hear all about my having tea with Kazuko at the Marunouchi Hotel, formulating plans for a women's section of the JBS, and she asked me what we were going to call it. I said we had not yet got around to that, but hoped to use the word *kai*, the Japanese word for 'club' to make the name itself Anglo-Japanese, although we are not a separate club, but a part of the JBS. And do you know, without a moment's hesitation she proffered, 'Elizabeth Kai!' Wasn't that amazing? I am quite sure Alice Morland's inspired name has much to do with our group's ever-growing popularity.

I shall never forget the very first outing of my group – a fascinating historical jaunt. It was arranged by group member Kazuko Shibata, whose family business was part of the history of old Tokyo. She recently authored a book entitled *Ginza Tailoring Establishment Yonedaya: Its first hundred years.* Our little group was ferried across a river to Tsukuda-jima, an island famous for the popular seafood relish called *Tsukuda-ni.* An old Hiroshige print shows the island being way out in Tokyo Bay, but it is almost part of the mainland now and a bridge is soon to supplant the ferry. We visited the island's ancient Sumiyoshi Shrine, whose high priest had been a colleague of Miss Shibata's, teaching English at Keio University. Afterwards, we dined on traditional chicken *mizutaki* at a famous old restaurant nearby. I remember that first outing vividly, and it was typical of the many interesting jaunts being thought up then by each group of members every month. One very imaginative group worked together making a quilt which they presented to Queen Elizabeth II when she and the Duke of Edinburgh visited Japan in 1975.

The Elizabeth Kai has gone from strength to strength, with now well over eighty members. We have had our fiftieth anniversary and are no longer in groups, because Japanese members now far outnumber British, so groups of half and half can no longer be formed! However, our enterprising and imaginative Committee, chaired by Kazuko's daughter, organize fascinating outings each month for everyone to enjoy together. Previously, the whole Elizabeth Kai only got together for the June Lunch and the October Tea.

Japanese wives now happily accompany their husbands to regular Japan-British Society occasions, and I cannot help wondering how much Japanese society in general has benefitted from the popularity of the Elizabeth Kai. Japanese women have always gathered together for a purpose such as working on a hobby, or visiting an exhibition, but the groups were usually confined to old friends from school days, whereas in the Elizabeth Kai they must make conversation with new friends; and so naturally many are the Anglo-Japanese friendships which have prospered. I like to think that the marvellous group in London's Japan Society called the *O-tomodachi Kai* (friendship club) was possibly inspired by our Elizabeth Kai. I believe groups in that London 'club' are simply pairs that change each year, and do things together, and hopefully become good friends.

I doubt if much has changed, though, regarding entertaining in the home. While in England 'a man's home is his castle', a man's home in Japan is his secret hide-away. Home is as private as a bedroom, and I think the Japanese still hesitate to entertain in it. Home is where one relaxes and need not be 'on show', and the only people one invites to one's home are generally relatives or extremely old and close friends. One reason for this attitude is that when Japanese entertain it is usually very formal. Special luxuries are provided and to offer potluck would be unthinkable. No loaf is better than half a loaf if it is to be offered to a guest, whereas we Westerners are much more casual and relaxed when we entertain. We are also more relaxed when we are *being* entertained.

CHAPTER 21

Marriage Customs

✦

PARTIES IN THE West have a valuable function because they provide a means for young men and women to learn to know each other with a view to getting married. Friendships between boys and girls form spontaneously and some of them lead to marriage. Young people try to be attractive and interesting companions in order to be popular. Finding a mate is up to the boys and girls themselves, usually with no outside help, although friends do like to introduce people to each other. But in Japan there has traditionally been so much outside help, that for this purpose, parties were not necessary at all. A matchmaker, called a *nakodo,* who can be a friend of the family, will suggest the names of several suitable mates, their backgrounds are carefully gone into, and if the girl or boy likes the idea of one of them as a prospective marriage partner, the two are formally introduced and date each other for a short while before making up their minds. If they decide against marriage, the *nakodo* will find another suitable candidate. There may not be the excitement of parties as we have them in the West, but it makes life much easier for the young people as they do not have to go through any social ordeals. Everyone gets married and there are no 'old maids'.

Nowadays, of course, Japanese boys and girls do often make friends with one another at work, at church, or at some other meeting place, and bypass the need for an introduction by the go-between; but a go-between can always be called in, and usually is, to help things along if the young man is bashful about proposing or the young girl somewhat shy about letting him know she likes him. And even if a go-between is not used at all, it is so traditional for one to be at the wedding that friends are often invited simply to fill that role as an honorary *nakodo.* My mother used to consider the Japanese matchmaker such a useful insti-tution that she thought it might well be adopted in the West. But nowadays, of course, in the West, there are newspapers, magazines and the internet which seem to offer plenty of introduction venues!

In Japan's traditional system the *miai,* or a little more politely *o-miai,* is the first formal meeting of a man and woman who have been suggested as suitable marriage partners by a third person. They date for a while, and then if the two are attracted to each other and decide to marry, the resulting marriage is called a *miai kekkon,* which is often translated as 'arranged marriage', but it is not an arranged marriage in the usual Western sense where the marriage must take place willy-nilly.

I had an *o-miai* once. It was set up for me by my best friend Wakako Okubo and her family. She began by asking me if I would like to have an *o-miai.* The man they had in mind was an American who was a colleague of her engineer uncle. Not knowing then how formal an *o-miai* was, and thinking it would just be merely a nice introduction to a congenial man I might enjoy meeting, I casually said 'yes'. But then the next day she rang to ask me if I was really sure I wanted to have an *o-miai,* and I wondered why she was worried, but replied again that I would be delighted. Then after seeking my confirmation once more, a meeting was arranged at the Imperial Hotel. We had a very formal tea in a small room, and there were about eight of us all told. He was a very pleasant man, and Wakako's uncle was there with his wife, and Wakako's elder sister and husband. We all had a very pleasant conversation over tea, and before breaking up, I invited my new friend to come down to Hayama one day. He came, and showed great interest in my shell collection, coming again several times, bringing containers he had very kindly made for my tiniest shells, which I had not known how to deal with. A year later Wakako's uncle phoned to ask how the friendship was going, and if he had asked me to marry him. He had not.

It was not until I had read Jun'ichiro Tanizaki's *The Makioka Sisters* that I discovered for the first time the very serious formality of an *o-miai*. Later, I ran into the man they had intended for me, at a party, and chatting about those days, I asked him if he had been aware of the formality of that meeting that had been arranged for us, and he said he too had had no idea how serious it was until much later, and we commiserated with each other at our joint rudeness in having treated it so casually. By that time I had heard that he was a homosexual!

Learning about homosexuals put an element of life for me into perspective, and I became quite an expert in recognizing men of that persuasion, since having remained single for quite a long time, I was always being introduced to single men that friends thought were just the ones for me. And alas, most of them were gaye. I have purposely put that 'e' at the end of the word. Although it does not change the sound, I like it spelled that way much better. That is the way I have now decided to spell it, since I think it is time Literature got the word 'gay' back again! I do so love Wordsworth's poem about daffodils, ending: 'A poet could not but be gay/ In such jocund company.'

But why do they *have* to be called anything special? And why do they have to be discriminated against? People who are attracted by the same sex should be no more a separated category than vegetarians,

RHYTHMS, RITES AND RITUALS

people who don't like cats or certain colours, etc., etc. I am enormously happy that gayes are now out of the closet with no further need to use girls like me for cover. My mother's cousin Isabella in Portland, Oregon, was a tragic victim, whose life was ruined. She had a 'boyfriend' who came to fetch her to go to parties, and they were so frequently seen together that everyone took it for granted they were lovers. I even said to her once, 'Why don't you marry Jimmy?' and tearfully she replied, 'He's never asked me.' Later I heard – from a gaye friend of mine from Portland – that Jimmy was one of a pair of gayes who lived together, and the other one also had a 'girlfriend' he was always with in public.

One of the times I was out of the country, there was a delightful English bank manager in Yokohama that my mother and her friends decided was 'just the man' for me, and when I got back she invited him to lunch to meet me. He had asked if he could bring a friend, and when they came in I was simply bowled over, not by him, but by his friend – an extremely handsome young Japanese man. I realized immediately that Neil was gaye. Not long afterwards the house next door to us became empty and Neil rented it and moved in. Neil and I were invited to many of the same parties in Tokyo, and at first I happily accepted his offer of a lift all the way there in his car, but afterwards I decided that always arriving together was not a good idea, and often purposely refused an invitation for that reason. But then I discovered that if I did not arrive at the party, he would take it upon himself to apologize on my behalf and say how sorry I was not to have been able to attend, making it sound as if we were living together. One sad part of it was he was such a nice person, and I did enjoy his company. He told me once he had only become gaye because his parents disapproved of his consorting with girls, but were delighted when he spent time with his male cousin! I think Japanese gayes who get married in the traditional way to satisfy their parents probably manage to carry on their male friendships on the side. But I fear poor Neil had his heart broken when his stunner got married.

The *o-miai* tradition certainly makes life easy for Japanese girls. A husband is found for them, and once they are married they are only expected to look after the house, carry out the family obligations, and bring up the children. They need not even be good cooks, for in Japan one can so easily have tasty food sent in or find it in the supermarket or convenience store. A Japanese wife does not have to entertain, nor does she have to hold her husband's interest, for all he requires is that she is gentle, obedient and uncomplaining. There is not much need for companionship since husband and wife do very little together. Their children are the principal bond, and on Sundays family outings are often planned for the sake of the children. It is also common for the father by himself to take the children to the zoo, for instance, to give the wife a holiday from them. Japanese mothers spend far more time with their children than most Western mothers do. For instance, they often even attend music lessons with their small offspring so that they can supervise their practice at home.

But Japanese women have one burdensome duty that Western women do not have: that of administering the family finances! The Japanese man brings home his pay and hands it to his wife who banks it, does the budgeting, all the paying and even gives the husband his allowance. They even deal with the family's income tax return. The reason for this is that in the old feudal times, merchants were third in the order of importance after the warriors and farmers, and money was considered rather sordid. So I suppose men today still consider that 'filthy lucre' is beneath them to handle!

I wrote 'brings home his pay-cheque' just now, but had to delete the word 'cheque' because hardly anyone uses them in Japan. I, personally, find that awfully inconvenient, because cheque stubs are such an easy record of payments. In Japan payments can be posted by putting cash in registered envelopes, but the most popular way is *furikomi:* depositing money electronically into bank accounts at a cash-point. But I find both methods tiresome to do, and the tiny receipts difficult to store efficiently for referring to later. I think the reason cheques have not been generally used in Japan is because seals and stamps are used to guarantee authenticity rather than signatures.

Apart from that, Japan has so many wonderful conveniences for making life easy. Baggage need never be trundled by hand if going on a trip, for numerous transport companies are there to do it for you at a reasonable price. Tipping is never required, so taxi rides and meals at restaurants are much more restful. Supermarkets and convenience stores have such a large variety of luscious ready-made meals that one seldom needs to do any cooking. The list goes on and on.

CHAPTER 22

Washoku and *O-furo*

✦

SPEAKING OF FOOD, traditional Japanese cuisine, *washoku,* was added to the UNESCO Intangible Cultural Heritage list in December 2013, as a 'valuable dietary culture nurtured by the Japanese people's soul, which respects nature'. My own discovery of *washoku* on returning to Japan in 1949 revolutionized not only my life, but my health as well. It may seem strange to readers in view of the initial thirteen years I spent here as a child, but the only Japanese food I had ever tasted was the cook's soy sauce I secretly licked in the kitchen when no one was looking, and the luscious

Japanese rice gruel, called *o-kayu*, flavoured with kelp and delectable shavings of dried bonito, made by my nanny, that I was allowed to have when not feeling well. I adored it, and it was well worth having a cold or a tummy upset in order to get it!

My American mother's year in China, where in those days foreigners were so terrified of picking up germs that they washed fruit and vegetables with strong antiseptics and germicides, made her feel that way about everywhere in the Far East, and she fed her family as much as possible on victuals imported by Caudrelier, Yokohama's French grocer, and cooked in the American way. Anything else was carefully washed in a pink liquid whose name escapes me. She even washed the money she handled, and we were the laughing stock of the neighbourhood for the bank notes seen drying on our clothes line!

As a child I did not enjoy Western food at all, except for the waffles we had every Sunday morning, the chocolate biscuits with white icing that we had when friends came for tea, and ice-cream with lots of chocolate sauce! My mother was awfully strict, and I was not allowed to leave the table until I had finished everything. I still remember sitting there day after day all alone until around 3 p.m., trying to deal with the cold lamb chops, and the mountain of tasteless cold vegetables, while my mother played Chopin preludes on the piano in the living room beyond. My English friends up on the Bluff often used to say they had had to go to bed without any supper because they had been naughty. So I used to try being naughty, but it did no good at all. No matter how naughty I was, my mother was a stickler for her idea of nourishment!

After we left Japan, beginning in Portland, Oregon, we stayed in many relative's and friend's houses in America, and by having to be polite and forcing myself to eat things I hated with a happy look on my face, I learned to appreciate Western cuisine a little better, but that was all, and I had lots of recurring digestive problems with both my stomach and bowels. But all those troubles disappeared in a flash when back in Japan, at long last, I finally discovered *washoku* for the very first time! I think Suzu Numano must have been right. I must be a Japanese, reincarnated in a Western skin! My favourite dish of all is sashimi, and its cousin sushi, which by now have taken the world by storm and have even entered the Oxford dictionary minus italics. But in 1949, the very idea of raw fish made Westerners squirm.

A young American couple I knew in the Occupation who had lived in Japan before the war and liked Japanese food, used to get Tokyo's leading sushi restaurant to set up a sushi bar in their house when they had a party. I was always invited, and I used to make a bee-line for that sushi bar. Once it was so crowded I could not get near it. They were all newcomers I had not seen before, and kept saying to one another, 'Gee isn't this good! What is it?' One of them turned around, saw me, and asked if I knew what it was. And I was mean. I said, 'It's raw fish'. They all looked horrified and quickly headed off, probably for the bathroom, to be sick, leaving me in sole possession of that delicious eatery.

So much is basically psychological! Raw fish does not sound very nice, and that is not what the Japanese call it. Sashimi just means 'sliced flesh'. It is like raw oysters that Westerners have been raving about for years. They do not call them 'raw oysters', do they? They call them 'oysters on the half shell'!

When my money-washing mother settled in Japan after having spent a year in pre-war China, little did she know that she had come to one of the cleanest nations in the world. My father used to say how impressed he had been when he first arrived in Japan to find how clean Japanese crowds were, with no unpleasant body odour. Many people even today in Europe who live in handsome and spacious houses consider a daily bath to be a luxury, and when they do take one, find it difficult to draw a deep enough one to cover the whole body. In Japan, however, the *o-furo,* a daily bath, is considered absolutely essential, and for centuries even the poorest woodcutter in his countryside hut has been able to soak up to the neck in a piping-hot tub of water every single night of his life. How did he do it, with no plumbing and very little fuel? He merely filled the tub twice a week and built a fire of kindling wood under the same water every evening. Since he would scrub himself thoroughly on an earthen floor covered with wooden planks before getting into the tub, the same water stayed clean enough for the whole family to soak in for many days. Moreover, the shape of the standard Japanese tub is far more efficient than its European counterpart. Instead of being long and shallow, the greater depth and smaller circumference of the Japanese tub enables a little hot water to cover a greater part of the body, as one sits upright with knees drawn up, and it is made of wood which does not cool the water as porcelain does.

After thoroughly warming his body in an extremely hot bath, the poor woodcutter then gets into a clean, pleasantly fresh bed. Japanese bedding, which is laid down on the floor matting every night and put away in cupboards in the daytime, is aired and sunned nearly every day. Comparing the life of this man with that of the vermin-infested royalty of eighteenth-century European palaces, who can say which knew the greatest bodily comfort?

For those Japanese whose flats and houses are too tiny to afford space for a bathtub, public bathhouses are available which are so pleasant that many citizens even prefer them to bathing at home. Two large piping hot Roman-style baths about two feet deep, one for men and one for women, provide a convivial meeting place, comparable to the village pub in England, and many are the people who look forward to their time of relaxation and pleasant gossip every evening in the public bath. On many Japanese streets in the evening, people can still be seen happily going to or from their bath, carrying a little basin and some soap and a towel. Showers and taps are provided outside the actual bath on a tiled floor, and one scrubs oneself thoroughly before entering the hot pools. Heretofore foreigners have been turned away from public baths for fear they will not conform to the rules. However, there is now a movement afoot to encourage them to come, as long as those with tattoos stay away, for in present-day Japan – the land where tattooing began – tattoos have become connected with the underworld!

Bathrooms in modern Japanese homes have tiled floors too, complete with drainage-pipe, and Japanese travellers are so used to their habit of pre-bath washing outside the tub, that hotels in the West sometimes come to grief as a result! The Japanese find it hard to understand how Westerners can bear to wash themselves 'in their own dirty water' as their saying goes. I am afraid my bathroom in Hayama was built in the English fashion, without a tiled floor, so I simply hope that if one bathes daily, in freshly drawn water, can the water be all that dirty? My father, in 1925 when our Hayama house – which he designed – was completed, sent for a traditional English bathtub with lion feet, in which I luxuriate to my heart's content. It is very comfortable, and is the only time I am completely relaxed, and that is where I do my best thinking. That is where I make my best translations of haiku. I lie back in the cosy heat of the water and juggle the words around in my mind until I get just what I want.

CHAPTER 23

My Royal Neighbours

✦

AFTER WORKING AT the embassy for three years, the British Council having opened in Tokyo, I was transferred to them as Librarian, so I had to quickly learn about the Dewey Decimal Classification System, although I had a wonderful Japanese assistant with a university degree in it. But at least I managed to give Prince Mikasa, Emperor Hirohito's youngest brother, a general idea of the system when he came to our British Council library and personally asked me to do so. The Prince, who specialized in ancient oriental history at Tokyo University, lectured in it afterwards at many universities in Japan, and is the honorary president of the Middle Eastern Culture Centre, which he established, as well as an honorary fellow of SOAS, the School of Oriental and African Studies in London.

It is truly impressive how academic the members of the Japanese Imperial family continue to be. Emperor Hirohito was already a budding scientist at the age of ten. His brother Prince Chichibu, in his book *Gotemba Tales,* describes how the two children went to the hills together to collect butterflies and insects, and that while he himself soon grew tired of checking each name, he says, 'not so Hirohito, who from beginning to end, no matter how many insects there were, carefully checked and recorded the name of every one'. At the age of seventeen, his discovery of a new species of deep-sea prawn was given the name *Sympathiphaea imperialis.* Having discovered over a hundred new species, His Majesty is ranked among the leading marine biologists of the world, and published three books detailing each of the following groups: the *Opistobranchia,* the *Ascidians,* and the *Crabs* of Sagami Bay, on which stands the Hayama Imperial Villa, at the opposite end of Isshiki Beach from us. We often watched, with interest, the long line of small open fishing boats containing His Majesty and large retinue row past our house. That was before the war. Afterwards he used but one medium-sized motor launch.

A job I was given not too long after my arrival at the Embassy was to ring chamberlain Kuroda at the Imperial Household to say that Emperor Hirohito's regular copy of the *Marine Zoological Record* had arrived from London, so would Kuroda-san please come to the Embassy and collect it. I had just learned how to drive, so when I called the chamberlain I offered to deliver the publication myself if that would be helpful. The chamberlain accepted with gratitude, saying he would arrange for me to enter the gate. I thought it was great fun driving into the Palace grounds as far as the Imperial Household office. Mr Kuroda and his family became very close friends. I even stayed with them in their house in Tokyo, and their lovely daughter Michiko, who worked at the Ministry of Foreign Affairs, often stayed with us in Hayama.

Emperor Hirohito's heart was most certainly not in the war, and I hate to think how many people abroad imagined he was actually directing it. The devoted marine zoologist tried to intimate his hatred of war at the first military conference he was required to attend by reciting his grandfather the Meiji Emperor's anti-war haiku:

It is our hope
That all the world's oceans
Be joined in peace;
So why do the winds and waves
Now rise up in angry rage?

(trans. by the Meiji Shrine Office)

Present-day Emperor Akihito too, in his 2013 Eightieth Birthday interview by the Press, underlined the importance of the post-war pacifist Constitution, and his son Crown Prince Naruhito, who turned fifty-four the same year, is reported by the *Japan Times* as having said: 'Today's Japan was built with the Constitution as the cornerstone, and our country is now enjoying peace and prosperity.'

Emperor Hirohito's marine zoological bent is also mirrored by his son, Emperor Akihito, who is engaged in making a study of the goby *(Gobiidae)* in his spare time. The Empress, too, is a scholar. She is very interested in books for children, and was the keynote speaker at the 26th Congress of IBBY the International Board on Books for theYoung held in New Delhi, India, in January 2012. She has translated from Japanese into English, and vice versa, many lovely books of verse for children. And besides that, she has a deep interest in the ancient imperial sericulture tradition. Her Majesty has not only carried on, but furthered with additional research, the ancient imperial custom of breeding silkworms that was initially reinstated by Haruko, the consort of the Meiji Emperor. Empress Michiko has especially developed a particular form of strong but very thin silk threads produced by a certain variety of silkworm called *koishimaru* which is valuable in restoring damaged silken antique imperial garments. Michiko-sama is also a pianist, whose professional stature was confirmed to me by a leading member of the Berlin Philharmonic Orchestra.

The members of the royal family are all musicians. Emperor Akihito plays the cello, and the Crown Prince the viola. In January 1993, the chamberlain phoned me to say Crown Prince Naruhito would very much like to come to my house and play the Mozart flute quartet if I could ask my Danish neighbour Marie Lorenz-Okabe to play the flute part and also find a violinist and cellist. Just before they were to arrive, the chamberlain phoned to say Her Majesty would also be coming. She brought some music to play on my piano, and I turned the pages for her. When they left, I overheard Empress Michiko say to her son, 'Hasn't it been fun! We can never do anything like this in Tokyo'.

I first met their Majesties at a dinner party at the British Embassy. After dinner, while we were having coffee and liqueurs in the drawing-room, I found myself sitting on the sofa with Empress Michiko. She is a graduate of the Sacred Heart University, and her English is perfect. 'Where do you live?' she asked me. When I said I lived in Hayama, Her Majesty asked where in Hayama. On 'Isshiki Beach,' I replied, and her face lit up. 'We are neighbours!' she said, delightedly. And when they next came down to their seaside Imperial Villa, I had a telephone call from a chamberlain asking if Her Majesty might visit me for tea, and could I please also invite the Danish flutist, Marie Lorenz Okabe. It seemed the Emperor and Empress, while walking back up to the Imperial Villa from the beach, had spoken to Marie, her Japanese architect husband, and young daughter, who had been standing outside their house, hoping to see the Royals go by! The Empress had met Marie at one of the Summer

Music Festivals in Karuizawa. We had a delightful chat over tea, and afterwards Marie and I entertained Her Majesty with my arrangement for flute, voice and Irish harp of *The Last Rose of Summer* in both English and Japanese. Empress Michiko plays the harp as well as the piano, and she then played and sang for us a charming lullaby she had composed. Several years later, both Their Majesties came for tea together. 'How lovely to listen to the sound of the sea,' said the Emperor. 'I imagine your Majesties must enjoy it at the Imperial Villa, too,' I said. 'No, we cannot hear it at all,' he replied. 'The concrete walls of the present building are much too thick.'

The original Imperial Villa was a beautiful old-fashioned Japanese edifice made of wood. According to historian Ben Ami Shillony, it had been acquired in 1894, during the reign of the Meiji Emperor, at the instigation of German doctor Erwin von Baelz, who served as physician to the Imperial Family. Dr von Baelz had discovered this seaside village and was impressed by its healthy climate and beautiful environment.

In 1971, three years after Boy and I had returned to Hayama following our marriage in Worthing, we were woken one night by a great crackling noise, and looked out of our bedroom window to see smoke and flames rising from the pine forest surrounding the Imperial Villa. It had been set on fire by a crazy youth who was annoyed because his aunt who lived nearby whom he had come to visit, was not at home. The caretakers had tried to put out the fire themselves, but by the time the Fire Department arrived the villa had burnt to the ground.

The *Goyotei* (imperial villa) was rebuilt in its present form ten years later, and I have been greatly honoured by their Majesties'company from time to time since then. Both Emperor Akihito and Empress Michiko are delightful people, so knowledgeable and so interesting, and so very kind.

CHAPTER 24

Two Composers

✦

WORKING FREELANCE NOW in Hayama I found many
of my childhood friends living permanently in their
summer villas, their Tokyo residences having burned
down in the wartime fire-bombing. Ikuma Dan, now
a well-known composer, was living with his second
wife in the family's summer villa directly across the
road, where as children we used to play. It had been
commandeered during the Occupation, but returned
to them afterwards. Meeting Ikuma again after all
those years we were amazed to discover we had
both become composers. He came over across the

road to call, bringing me a copy of his lovely opera *Yuzuru*, which he had autographed 'With memories of hide-and-seek'. It was hard to believe he was the little boy I had first met in a futon closet while playing 'sardines'. It was astounding to find we were now both music composers! My cantata *And Certain Women Followed Him* had just had its initial performance at the Occupation's Chapel Centre in Tokyo, and a tape of it was still on my tape-recorder, so I played it for him.

I offered to translate the libretto of Ikuma's opera *Yuzuru* (The Twilight Heron) into English, so he came back again next day and we started work on it down on the beach, sitting on the sand. After working on it for quite some time, Ikuma suggested we have a break and take a stroll along the beach at the water's edge. There is a low, narrow promontory at the end of Isshiki Beach, opposite the Imperial Villa. In those days it had a grove of pine trees surrounding a small Imperial summer tea pavilion with a view of Mount Fuji that Mrs Vining, his tutor, wrote in her *Windows for the Crown Prince,* was the very best view of that mountain. We climbed up onto the Imperial headland and sat down with our backs against the pavilion's bamboo fence, and engaged in a long chat about the intervening years since we were children. 'It's amazing,' Ikuma said, as we began ambling back, 'how our thoughts seem to roll along together, like two little pebbles side by side on a slope!' We had found we were, indeed, incredibly compatible.

I continued translating his opera, working together on it much of the time, since we lived so near one another. Its title *Yuzuru* raised quite a problem concerning music and language: whether to translate *tsuru* correctly as 'crane' or change the bird to 'heron'. *Yuzuru* actually means 'Evening Crane' but I translated the title as *The Twilight Heron*, because 'crane' is not a pretty word to sing, with its three sounds squashed into a single syllable, whereas the Japanese word for crane is *tsu-ru* which is simple and beautiful to sing. As a musician, Ikuma well appreciated the advantage of the two-syllable 'he-ron' to be sung to his music for the two-syllable *'tsuru'*. However, Junji Kinoshita, author of the play Ikuma had used for his libretto, was very unhappy at my changing the bird, since it was based on a famous old folk tale. The three of us had dinner together to discuss it. Kinoshita also pointed out that *sagi,* the Japanese for 'heron', sounds the same as the Japanese word meaning 'swindler', which he did not like. I countered that by telling him that in English crane had also the meaning of an ugly machine for moving heavy objects! But I am now not sure at all that I made the right decision, and wish I had kept the word 'crane', for I have become a great crane enthusiast, and even wrote a book about it, called *The Japanese Crane: Bird of Happiness.*[1]

A truly wonderful collaboration ensued for Ikuma and me. I was instrumental in the publication of *The Twilight Heron* by Boosey & Hawkes in London.

---

[1] *The Japanese Crane: Bird of Happiness*, Dorothy Britton (Author), Tsuneo Hayashida (Photographer), Kodansha International Ltd. Revised edition, 1995.

I translated two more of his operas, as well as a volume of Ikuma's collected songs. And later I translated into English and read for him his fascinating talk to the Asiatic Society of Japan on The Influence of Japanese Traditional Music on the Development of Western Music in Japan, which is in Vol. 8 of Series 3 of the Society's *Transactions*. Ikuma on his part conducted performances of my music for me, since I had never properly learned how to conduct. He even re-wrote for me the music for one of the songs in a musical I composed, because, believe it or not, he said I had not got the rhythm quite right for the Japanese words! And he was wonderfully kind in introducing me to influential people in the Japanese music world.

Besides composing, Ikuma was a talented essayist, writing a regular piece called *Pipe Smoke* in the Asahi newspaper's magazine *The Asahi Graph*. He was also a poet, and translated into Japanese my *Three Sea Hymns* for unaccompanied voices, which were published in Number 5, Volume 2 of Japan's *Gasshokai*, (Choral Club) magazine. The first and third sea hymns are my own poems, which are even better in Ikuma's beautiful Japanese.

1. The Sea

All praise and honour be to Thee,
O God, who made the wondrous sea,
And so much beauty all around;
O how Thy goodness doth abound,
O God who made the sea!

Sea-horses, and coral dragons,
Argonaut, and pearly nautilus;
Such gems are laid for me upon the shore!
And limpid as the fishes swim,
Exulto Deo is my hymn!

2. Shells

I will praise Thee, O Lord,by the sea!
Bring me a psaltery studded with shells,
Find me a conch on the silent gray sands,
For I will praise Thee O Lord, by the sea,
Underneath the cathedral hills.

The libretto of my cantata was written by a very talented American artist, specializing in portraits, called
Elizabeth Baskerville, who was the wife of General
McNaughton, Air C-in-C at SCAP. I had met her
through Boy, who knew the General at the time of
the Korean War. When Beth showed me her libretto, I was very eager to set it to music. Her theme
was that it was the women who first listened to Jesus
and followed him right from the beginning, without ever faltering like Peter, who denied him thrice.
Beth became one of my dearest friends, and would
come down to Hayama time and time again to stay
while I was working on the music, and she was there
when I first knew the adult Ikuma. She happened
to be looking out of the upstairs bathroom window
one day and saw Ikuma arrive and noticed that he
carefully combed his hair before knocking on the
front door. 'Dorothy,' she said, 'I think he must be

in love with you.' I blushed, for I was in love with him. He had been married twice, and his second wife, Kazuko, was pregnant, and I had told him we must not see too much of one another. But he said Kazuko had told him she wanted to divorce him, and he said he wanted to marry me, and assured me her baby would not be a problem since he knew that if necessary I would look after the baby, as if it were my own, because I was such a kind person! I believed him, and went on seeing him a great deal. He took me everywhere with him, even when he was conducting background music for movies, because he said he wanted me to meet all his musician friends and colleagues.

One day, Beth McNaughton brought me a letter she had received from Ikuma's father, Baron Ino Dan. In it the Baron asked her to do what she could to try and stop me marrying his son. 'I know it will only end in great tragedy,' he wrote, 'and poor Dorothy will be swept up in it as if by an enormous tsunami.' Perhaps there had been trouble when he left his first wife. But it is difficult to separate lovers, and we were so compatible, and had become so very fond of each other.

Then, at a symphony concert given by the *San-nin no Kai,* (The Group of Three), where symphonies by Dan, Hiraizumi and Akutagawa were being performed, Kazuko angrily confronted me and ordered me to stop seeing her husband. She went on to tell me he had told her I would care for her baby, but she angrily said she refused to have someone of a different hair colour bringing up her child. I was staggered, wondering what to do, and I can not remember what exactly happened immediately after that. Ikuma's mother, the Baroness, liked me a lot, and would have liked to have me in their family. So did his sister who was married to the head of the Bridgestone Tyre company, and they offered to let him use a bungalow they had in Hayama. I am sure my own mother would have been in favour of the marriage too, if Ikuma had been single, having known his grandparents before the war. But the Baroness did warn me of one thing. She said her son could be violent, and had once struck her.

Ikuma moved out of his house and into the offered bungalow, and I spent quite a lot of time there with him – but never overnight for fear of upsetting my mother! I even taught him chess, which he became quite good at. It was there that I encountered his violence. In fact I thought he was going to kill me. One day, Ikuma had said, 'Let's be mature in our relationship, and never be upset if either of us mentions someone we have loved.' So I took him at his word, and in our conversation I once casually mentioned Boy – whom he already knew about – and he erupted in a colossal spate of jealousy and started beating me with a very large, heavy fishing rod. I finally managed to escape and ran out into the driveway and hid in the hedge. Ikuma followed me out but could not find me, and I saw him open the door of my car to try and incapacitate it, but not knowing how to drive, all he did was pull out the cigarette lighter and throw it away, seemingly satisfied that it had put the starter out of action. Directly he was back in the house I leapt into the car and drove home. While escaping from the fishing-rod attack, my clothes became torn, and my head was suffering badly from concussion. I told my mother we had been for a walk and I had missed my step in the dark and had fallen down a cliff. After a while the telephone rang, and it was Ikuma, who made an abject apology and said he was terrified that I would stop loving him. Being a very forgiving person, I forgave him. He then called a taxi and came and apologized a whole lot more in person.

CHAPTER 25

London and Paris

✦

WHILE AT MILLS, I had continued my study of piano at the San Francisco Conservatory, and had given a recital there before leaving, including playing several of my compositions. My teacher had urged me to study with Myra Hess in London, but what with meeting my then intended, breaking up with him and joining the BBC, I never got around to applying for lessons with Myra Hess, famous for her lunchtime concerts at the National Gallery during the war, surrounded by famous paintings. So my mother thought I should take a trip back to London for that purpose.

She may have also thought it wise to get me away from Japan for a while.

But Ikuma told me he would come and see me in London, because he was attending the Cannes film festival in France. My mother and I sailed from Yokohama on 21 April 1956 on the *Chusan*. Our five-week journey to England by sea – still then the normal way to travel – was tremendous fun. It was the first time I had ever been through the Suez Canal and the Mediterranean. My mother and I were joined at our table by D.J. Enright, with his terrific sense of humour, and his French wife and little girl. He had been Japan's resident British poet following after Edmund Blunden and G.S. Fraser. Pianist Yoshiko Okami, joined us too. She had been told to look me up by Wakako Okubo's violinist brother who had been a fellow student with her at the Tokyo Conservatory; and then there was a young man from the British Embassy as well, who spent every other minute writing to his fiancée, whom he was on the way home to marry. At the usual farewell ball on the last night the six of us wore our summer kimonos, called *yukata,* and won a prize for singing and dancing the popular Kyushu Coal Miner's Song, for which I happened to have the music, and which the band played for us magnificently.

Two ladies we had known at Dolphin Square had bought a house in St John's Wood, and were renting rooms in it. We took the ground floor flat, and when Ikuma Dan arrived in London after the film show at Cannes on the Riviera, where a Japanese film with music by him was being shown, I suggested he rent a single room that happened to be vacant in the same house where Mother and I were staying. While in London he needed to have a lot of dental work done and I introduced him to my dentist. While there, he wrote up his London visit for his regular *Asahi Graph* essay, cleverly calling it by a Japanese homonym, *rondon no hanashi* which can either mean 'Talking about London' or 'Toothless in London'. The Japanese language lends itself to hilarious word play!

My cousin Gordon Daniels, on my father's mother's side, was a student at the London School of Economics at that time, and we took him out to supper one evening at a restaurant off Oxford Street. Ikuma came with us. When introducing Ikuma to Gordon, Mother explained how his grandfather, Baron Takuma Dan, had been assassinated by a rightist while he was taking a visiting British dignitary to the Kabuki Theatre in the interests of furthering Anglo-Japanese friendship. Gordon was intrigued, and during the conversation that evening, he became so fascinated with my mother's explanation of Japanese history, that he changed the subject of his studies at the university, and is now one of Britain's leading authorities on Anglo-Japanese history! Just another example of how one thing leads to another, and how intertwined people's karma is.

Unfortunately, the famous pianist Myra Hess was not able to take me on as a pupil, and I only visited Edmund Rubbra a few times – the composer cum pianist she thought it would be ideal for me to study with – but the place where he lived was extremely difficult to get to, and practising on the piano in our flat turned out to be impossible, because the neighbours complained. It was all so discouraging, that I more or less gave up trying to become a performer on the piano, and decided to simply concentrate on composition instead.

While we were in London, my mother heard from her old friends the Hailes who had given my parents their wedding reception in Shanghai in 1920, to say their daughter and son-in-law, Kate and John Payne, were in Paris, and would like me to visit them. I had never been to Paris and accepted gladly. John was a Colonel in the US Army. He was very nice, but Kate was so cynical, and critical all the time of everything in Paris, that I did not enjoy Paris at all. She made Paris seem a very depressing place. After spending several days with them, I was planning to spend a week with Angela, my best friend at Mills College, where we were the only two British girls. When I joined Angela at her favourite hotel, Paris suddenly became a completely different city! She of course spoke French and so did I, and she loved Paris very much, and I began to love it too! It is amazing how psychological so many things are! And then Ikuma arrived in Paris, and he and I, and Angela and her boyfriend, we all four had such a happy time together. Ikuma was a chain-smoker, and had been wanting to translate into Japanese a well-known English book about pipes and smoking, so I decided to stay on in

Paris with Ikuma for a while. We moved into a nice little inn and worked on the book together.

Back in London, some distant Scottish cousins whom my mother had discovered on the Duncan side of her family tree – the Drummonds of Megginch, who were closely connected to the Duncans of Seaside – had lost their mother, and hoped she and I could attend the funeral at Megginch Castle in Perth. Ikuma was planning to attend the Edinburgh Festival, so after the funeral I joined him there.

CHAPTER 26

Harps and Angels

✦

AT THE EDINBURGH Festival, I was enthralled by a young singer of old Irish songs with an Irish harp. After returning to Japan, I had contemplated for a while the idea of using the *biwa*, Japan's equivalent of the lute, for accompanying my folksongs. The *biwa* is almost the oldest Japanese musical instrument, arriving from China around the seventh century. With its beautiful shape and warmth of tone I thought it would be an intriguing change from the ukulele and guitar. I even had one made for me, but the Japanese lady who kindly arranged that was so determined that

I should learn to play it properly in the traditional Japanese manner – which she said would take many, many years to master – that I became too embarrassed to say that I wanted to work out how to play it in my own fashion!

The Irish harp seemed even better for my folk songs. I was thoroughly converted. Back in London the very first thing I did was find a maker and ordered an Irish harp. They were interested when I said I was taking it back to Japan, for they said a leading Japanese koto player had just bought one of their harps. And now, would you believe it, there are more Irish harps being made in Japan that anywhere else in the world. And there are lots of harpists, too. When they are learning they buy Irish harps to practise on. I am the only one in Japan who just uses it for accompanying folk songs in the traditional Irish way.

When harps first reached England at the time of the Crusades, they were small, and were called English harps. But the English did not take to them, and preferred the lute, also a result of the Crusades, for the Middle East seems to have been the birthplace of many musical instruments.

I had a funny time getting my harp back to Japan. After collecting it at the maker's, taxis would not stop for me. When one finally did, I asked the driver if he had any idea why nobody seemed to want to stop for me. 'You'll see,' he replied. And sure enough, before long, the driver of a taxi going by shouted at mine, 'Ya won't need that where *you're* goin'.' In those days London taxis had an open section for luggage on the left of the driver, so the harp, in its case, was visible. My driver knew that sooner or later he was sure to be reminded by a passing colleague that it is only angelic people when they die that end up sitting on clouds playing harps! Much later, at one of the airports, they rushed me onto the plane saying, 'That harp'll frighten the other passengers', and hid my instrument behind the coats!

Later on, finally back in Japan, I thankfully found there was no connection there between harps and angels! But I had a different problem. The Irish girl at the Edinburgh Festival sat on a little milking stool, and the nearest small, low stool I could find in Tokyo was the kind they use in public baths, but Ikuma said Japanese audiences would be shocked to see a musician playing a harp sitting on a bath stool! But fortunately I discovered that the koto player who bought that Irish harp in London and went on to manufacture them in Japan, had developed legs for the harps, so they put legs on mine for me too!

While still in London, I heard from G. Schirmer in New York, that my cantata was ready for publication and they hoped I could call in there on my way back to Japan to read the proofs. My resourceful mother, while shopping in London, had seen a notice in the window of the Cunard Line office offering a very reasonable trip on the *Caronia* as far as New York, from where a cruise of the Caribbean was to begin – and moreover, it was going to New York via Bermuda! We were thrilled with the idea of seeing all our dear Bermuda friends again. We sailed on

2 January 1957, and arrived in Hamilton on the 10th. The Butterfields insisted we stay with them, which we did for about two weeks. We flew from Bermuda on the 27th to New York, where the music editor at Schirmer kept telling me how much he liked my cantata. While in New York I had some harp lessons. I also wanted to see my dear friend Elizabeth Butterfield, now divorced and living in Baltimore, but there was a blizzard which prevented my getting there. I never saw her again. I had several long conversations with her on the telephone. She sounded lonely and unhappy, and was drinking far too much.

My mother and I then flew to San Francisco where her bigoted eldest brother Henry met us with the words, 'What's this I hear about Dorothy going to marry a window-cleaner?' He was the one who greeted the news of Mother's marriage to my English father with, 'Have you lost your mind, marrying a foreigner in a heathen land?' And now the 'foreigner' was Japanese, and he remembered how in California's early days so many poor Japanese immigrants had to work at low-class jobs like washing windows! Uncle Henry must have heard from the Paynes about my being with Ikuma in Paris.

While Mother stayed with her favourite youngest brother Stanley and his pianist wife Opal in Berkeley, I went to visit my dear friend Beth McNaughton, author of the libretto of my cantata. She had left Japan with her husband, and was then living in Los Angeles. I had a tape-recording with me that I was looking forward to playing for Beth. Of the many musical scores I had composed for documentaries produced by Ian Mutsu's International Motion Picture Company for introducing Japan abroad, one of them, 'Garden of Three Glens' describing Yokohama's famous Sankeien Park, won a prize. So when the Tokyo National Art Gallery had asked Ikuma Dan to compose the background music for their new film *Edo jidai no bijutsu* (Art of the Yedo Period), Ikuma apparently told them how adept I was at composing music for documentaries, and suggested they approach *me*. It was a beautiful film, and when I happily carried out the request, Ikuma conducted the performance by a small chamber-music group, and the sound was so pleasant that just for fun, I had arranged the music into a five-movement suite I called *Yedo Fantasy,* which I put on a tape, little knowing what it would lead to!

At the McNaughtons, a friend of theirs suggested I show it to Capitol Records, who immediately snapped it up for use in their 'Music of the World' series, providing I composed enough further music to fill up an LP! So while visiting my cousin Patsy, who lived nearby, I started a second five-movement suite which I called *Tokyo Impressions*. I completed it when I was back in Tokyo, and Ikuma got an orchestra together to perform it for me, with himself conducting. Capitol's LP, entitled 'Japanese Sketches' came out later that same year, and was hailed by the *American Record Guide* as a highly successful 'translation of the koto-samisen aesthetic into Occidental terms!' But I was disappointed with the cover photo Capitol chose of Japanese children watching a travelling storyteller's show. It seemed so utterly inappropriate. I showed them a lovely photograph I had hoped they would use of pine trees leaning over the Imperial Moat, since one of the movements of *Tokyo Impressions* is called *Evening on the River Sumida,* but they told me not even Frank Sinatra is allowed to pick his own cover design!

CHAPTER 27

Back to Work in Japan

✦

PUBLISHED COPIES OF my cantata *And Certain Women Followed Him* arrived from Schirmer's not long after my return to Japan. It was soon performed in Tokyo by NHK, the Japan Broadcasting Corporation. They sang it beautifully in English after I personally coached the soloists and chorus. That same year Ikuma had it translated into Japanese with the title *Gariraya no Onna-tachi* (Women of Galilee) and it was performed in Nagoya by CBC, the Central Broadcasting Corporation, conducted by Ikuma. I had purposely begun my cantata with a tenor recitative sung in the style of the Psalms from the Church of England's *Book of Common Prayer*, but Ikuma felt the need of an introductory prelude, so he made a lovely orchestration of my a capella chorus, for that purpose.

One of the singers Ikuma had recruited for that Nagoya performance had such a lovely mezzo-soprano voice that back in Tokyo I got her to sing my new composition *Chinoiserie* for voice and string quartet. Its opening poem by Gautier begins:

Ce n'est pas vous, non, madame, que j'aime,
Ni vous non plus, Juliette ni vous,
Ophélia, ni Béatrix, ni même
Laure la blonde, avec ses grands yeux doux.

Celle que j'aime, à present, est en Chine;

The genders are reversed, but I composed it to subtly express the fact that I was in love with an oriental. Many years later it was brought out as a CD in New York by Arabesque, played by the Portland String Quartet and sung by Rita Noel.

Back to work, I composed more film scores of various sorts, including the background music for *My Garden Japan,* an award-winning American film about Japanese gardens produced by the International Minerals and Chemical Corporation, a well-known fertilizer company, which was shown continuously at the Expo'67 World Fair in Canada. I wanted to use mainly *gagaku* instruments, and Ikuma introduced me to the Imperial court musicians, many of whom are descendants of the original families who came from China and Korea in the sixth century. The *gagaku* instrument I like best is the *wagon*. A small, koto-like zither with only six strings, which is said to have predated the other kotos and may even be indigenous. It has a lovely tone, very much like an Irish harp, and so I composed a beautiful melody for it. The man who played it had tears in his eyes, saying it was the first time he had ever played a melody. He said that in the *gagaku* court orchestra he normally only plays just a single roll stroke across the strings from time to time!

I also had several weekly radio programmes on NHK's Radio Japan, transmitted in English to all parts of the world intended to spread abroad knowledge of the country's culture. One of my programmes was on folklore, and consisted of dramas I wrote and directed, based on Japanese traditional folk tales. Another was called 'Let's Sing in Japanese' and introduced the most traditionally popular folk songs, lyric songs and children's songs. They were sung by Aiko Anzai, a well-loved singer known as *uta no obasan* (The Singing Auntie) which I, as narrator, translated and explained. Twenty-four of the songs were published by NHK in a beautiful volume with illustrations by the modern wood-block print artist Kiyoshi Saito. A further volume in the same format was published a year later with twenty folk songs for which I composed the piano accompaniments. 'Let's Sing in Japanese' was such a popular programme, it was continued for four years. The

American Embassy Women's Club asked us to perform for them at their meeting in the Tokyo Hilton Hotel, where we ended it with everyone singing and dancing that jolly *tanko-bushi* the Coal Miner's Song from Kyushu, in which Mrs Shoda, the mother of Empress Michiko, joined us!

From 1958, for twelve years, I had a regular television programme on NHK called Junior High English Classroom, which was beamed to all the schools. It was twenty minutes long, fifteen minutes teaching English, and always finishing with a Scottish, Irish or English folk song, accompanying myself on the Irish harp.

First, I used to go through the words of the song line by line, asking the schoolchildren listening to repeat them after me. It was the method I had learned from the French nun forty years earlier. But not nearly so potent, of course, since it was not possible to continue the repetitions enough times to be *really* effective! But I keep meeting people who watched my programme as young students and at least they seem to have enjoyed it and found it interesting. In those days I was often deluged by whole classes of students visiting temples who wanted my autograph. I remember once overhearing a woman noticing them who said to her companion: 'I don't know who she is, but we'd better get her autograph anyway!'

Boys and girls on school excursions are a common sight in Japan. And when they see a foreigner they usually all start yelling *Ha-raw, ha-raw* at the top of their voices, and it sounds just like the *haro chuiho* (big wave warning), down at the beach when a big storm or tsunami is feared. How I wish those boys and girls could call out a friendly *'hullo, hullo!'* getting their 'l' and 'o' sounds right, instead of turning their greetings into a scary tsunami warning!

One Christmas, the producers of my Junior High English Classroom thought it would be fun to ask the listeners to send Miss Britton a Christmas Card. I was horrified at the idea of having to respond to hundreds of greetings. But they assured me I would not have to deal with even a single one, for they planned simply to send back a postcard with a photograph of me and my harp and containing a printed message. Then, one day, a parcel arrived from the Broadcasting Corporation enclosing some remarkably delightful hand-painted cards with imaginative messages on each of them in excellent English, with a note saying the producers thought these were so out of the ordinary that they simply could not resist sending them for me to see. They were from a school in Kochi, one of the four provinces of Shikoku (Four Province) Island, the smallest of Japan's four main islands.

I also was amazed by those beautiful Christmas cards, and sent them off to Isabel Rendell, my English first cousin once removed – the daughter of my father's cousin Anna Bannister. I sent them to Isabel because she was a teacher at a famous old school called Hugh Sexey's Church of England Middle School in Wedmore, Somerset, and I thought it would be a marvellous opportunity for her to get some of her pupils to become international pen-friends with the senders of the cards. Isabel was interested, and made an enthusiastic start. Quite a few of her pupils sent off letters, but replies from Japan were apparently very slow in coming, for although their teacher in Kochi tried hard, the Japanese children just could not think what to write about and how to say it, and found the whole exercise too frightfully daunting. In despair, the Japanese teacher of the English class, Noriko Fukuju, wrote to Isabel to explain, and in doing so found it so much fun to have an English pen-friend herself, that a tremendous friendship began between the two teachers.

Eventually, Noriko saved up enough money to travel to England, and managed to take the train down to Yeovil in Somerset, where Isabel and her sister Joan then lived. While staying there with the Rendell girls, Noriko kept writing letters and post-cards to all her friends in Kochi. Isabel offered to show her the nearby postbox, which was inserted in the cliff and hard to see. But Noriko, who had been strolling about the neighbourhood, assured Isabel she had seen it, and had already posted her letters.

Soon after Noriko had left for home, Isabel noticed in the local newspaper a headline: 'STRANGE MISSIVES COME THROUGH PUB'S LETTER BOX'. The name of the pub was 'The Quicksilver Mail', at the top of Hendford Hill, on which Joan and Isabel lived, halfway up. Isabel realized it must have been Noriko's letters in Japanese, and that Noriko must have thought The Quicksilver Mail was a Post Office. The pub was very old, and was said to have had a connection – perhaps it was a stopping-over place – with the *Quicksilver*, a famous mail-carrying horse-drawn coach that was put on the road in 1820 and made the journey from London to Devonport, near Plymouth, in twenty-one hours and fourteen minutes including stops! It was known not only for its speed but also for its beautiful looks, which appealed to artists. Isabel went in and explained to the pub owner about Noriko, and Noriko got their address from Isabel and wrote to them apologizing for having mistaken them for a Post Office. Noriko and the pub owners are still in touch!

It was exciting for me when my Capitol Records LP came out the year following my return to Japan after that sojourn abroad. What happened next was my greatest thrill of all. That music of mine was used for the Nagoya Odori! Nagoya's Koizaburo Nishikawa was one of the leaders in *nihon buyo* the traditional Japanese dance. He thought it would be a change to choreograph his annual geisha dance show that year to Japanese-style music played on Western, rather than Japanese musical instruments. To achieve this, he went to CBC, and went through all of their gramophone records, and the only one that fit the bill exactly was my *Japanese Sketches*!

He used my music again the year after that at the Akasaka Odori, one of the geisha shows in Tokyo, as well as commissioning a brand new piece for a geisha dance called 'Snow, Moon and Flowers' performed at the famous Kabuki Theatre, which to me was a tremendous thrill. If only my father could have known! I can not help wondering if I am the first foreigner to have been asked to write music for *nihon buyo*. And even more exciting, Nishikawa asked me to compose the score for a musical. The story, by a well-known Japanese writer, was very amusing – all about a beggar woman sitting on a street corner, who is really a millionaire, to whom all the town toffs are in debt. It was set in China, so I went to Hong Kong to learn about Chinese music, since I wanted my music for *Madame Beggar* to have a truly Chinese feel. Its performances in 1959 were hailed as a very special and novel *nihon buyo* attraction.

CHAPTER 28

Dreaming of Elephants

✦

IN JULY 1961, I had a fascinating dream. In it I looked out of my bedroom window, and saw that a young elephant I had bought at a bargain sale and tied to one of the pine trees in our garden, had got away, and had joined four other young elephants down on the beach. Other people must have gone to the same bargain sale, I thought. Then, still in my dream, I noticed that the rock that juts out over the sand towards the sea in front of our house had turned into the bow of a ship. It was in fact a preview of a scene I was to see in a fortnight's time!

On 8 July, Sir Vere and Lady Redman asked me to drop in for a drink. He had been knighted on his retirement, and they were leaving Japan the following week, and they wondered if I could be induced to join them on the voyage. The ship was a French merchant ship that only took four passengers, they said, and one place was vacant. They were sailing to London via Saigon, and would be stopping off in many unusual ports. It appealed to me greatly. We would be speaking French most of the time. It was not until we were en route that they let me know that it was my mother's idea to get me away from Japan again for a while so I could carefully think over my relationship with Ikuma.

The ship was called the *Maori,* and on the 27th I joined it in the port of Shimizu in Shizuoka Prefecture, about 600 kilometres south of Hayama. After visiting three ports in Taiwan, we spent three days in Hong Kong before landing in Saigon, where we took on five young elephants! I had completely forgotten my dream until we set off for Singapore, where we were going to have dinner with the Enrights, for the English poet was now teaching there. I was standing on the upper deck with the Redmans and the French lady who was my cabin-mate, gazing out to sea, and I suddenly realized it looked just exactly the way the rock below my bedroom window had seemed to resemble a ship's bow in my dream, and instead of on Isshiki beach, the five young elephants were there below us on the *Maori's* deck! Amazing, wasn't it, for when I dreamed that dream little did I know I would soon be travelling on a ship to Vietnam. I read somewhere that dreams were often mixtures of the future as well as of the past.

Four of the elephants were in simple shacks built there on the deck for them before we sailed, as we watched. A fifth shack was built too, but the elephant it was for kept destroying it, so finally they had to let it remain free. The crew called that difficult elephant *le voleur* (the bandit). But it was a kind-hearted rogue. The Vietnamese who was in charge of the elephants fed them daily from a large pile of sugar-cane up in the bow, and as a treat he occasionally gave each one a banana. One day he left a whole bunch of bananas lying on the hatch, and before Bandit stole some for himself he first carried the bananas over to the shacks so that his cloistered friends could each have one too. It was a most touching sight. One of the elephants in the shacks was a baby elephant, and as we neared Europe with its cooler climes, the poor baby suffered from a chill and had a runny nose, and the keeper kept treating it with antibiotics. Soon after we arrived in England the newspaper reported the discovery of a baby elephant's carcass washed up on a shore of the English Channel. I think it was probably our little baby, and felt very sad.

We arrived in London on 7 September at the King George V Dock at five in the afternoon, and I made my way to the Drummonds house where I was to stay. Dozens of wonderful letters from Ikuma were there awaiting me. He told me how much he loved me and missed me, and how he had hated my going away, but thanked me for my accounts of the trip which I had posted from every port, so that he could picture me in his mind on the ship with those young elephants, as well as each of the fascinating places we stopped at – Saigon, Singapore, Djibouti, Tunis, Gibraltar, Casablanca. . . . And he told me how lonely he was in the Bridgestone cottage, and how he could hardly wait for me to come back and join him there. They were intensely romantic letters, written in Japanese in *romaji* (Roman letters), recalling in detail how beautifully we had made love together in Paris, and describing how he hoped we would make love again in future in Hayama at the lovely cottage – even perhaps singing a madrigal together at the same time! How delightful, I thought. When I took him to meet Norman Mansbridge in his London flat, we must have told Ikuma about singing madrigals while treading water in the bay in Bermuda!

While in England on my own I was eager to learn more about my father's family, so I took a train to Yeovil to visit cousins Joan and Isabel Rendell. There I saw a painting Joan had made of the house in Elmdon where my father had lived as a child. Joan had copied it from a drawing made by her mother, his cousin Anna, who had actually been there. Joan very kindly let me have it. I took it with me when I went to stay with the Mansbridges at Oak Cottage, in Bardfield End Green, in Dunmow, near Thaxted in Essex, who had promised to take me to their butcher, Vic Britton, to find out what he knew.

During the war many young RAF cadets were sent to America to train. My old friend Eleanor Poole from Boston met one of them and fell in love. But nobody was ever considered good enough for her by her mother, so in desperation, Eleanor came over to London determined to marry the young man willy-nilly. That was in 1956 when Mother and I were in London living in Dolphin Square. I offered to help Eleanor find a home for them to live in, and we went together to various estate agents. We had not had much luck, and were getting rather discouraged, when we noticed a number of agents called Britton & Poole. I suggested that if we went into one of them and I said I am Miss Britton, and this is Miss Poole, the amazing coincidence of the two names might just make them take an interest in helping us. Just then we passed one, but our bus kept going on and on. It did not stop for such a long time, that we did not feel like walking all that way back. And since it was a bit of a joke anyway, we let it go. It turned out that the Britton of the firm of estate agents called Britton & Poole was my father's half brother! Wasn't that amazing? A man I did not even know existed. My father had never even told us that his father had married again. If only we had gone in to that firm of estate agents, the owner would doubtless have been thrilled. But by the time I finally discovered the fact, he had died.

CHAPTER 29

Finding the Brittons

✦

I SPENT A delightful week with the Mansbridges, in their charming home called Oak Cottage in Bardfield End Green. The house had previously been owned by George Morrow (1869–1955) the *Punch* artist who did those marvellous historical drawings, and it had a fascinating series of them all the way down the stair-case. When Norman was in Bermuda, he had told me about their butcher in Thaxted whose name was Britton, spelled the same as mine, and had wondered if he might be a relative. They took me to his shop and I asked the proprietor, Victor Britton, if he knew anything about my grandfather John Britton. He said, 'Yes, John James was a cousin of my father's and he owned the pub in Elmdon!' I had no idea that the house in Elmdon, the drawing of which Joan Rendell had given me, was a pub! Vic offered to take us there. The pub called *The Wilkes Arms,* was in the process of being turned into an attractive residence by a couple returning from abroad, who had bought it. I also asked Vic if I could see the church in Elmdon where my father used to help the organist by working the bellows. My father had told me how he had even taught himself to play, by carefully watching the organist, and that he used to fill in as organist himself, when necessary, although still a child. We looked in the graveyard, too, and found the grave of my grandmother. It was all very exciting.

Victor George 'Vic' Britton was a delightful man, and a very superior butcher, for he had a farm and raised his own cattle. He was also a fine horseman, and a member of the local hunt before fox-hunting was banned. He suggested I go and see his Uncle George, Postmaster of Haywards Heath, who was the person who knew most about the family. 'Uncle' George replied thus, dated 13 December 1961, to the letter I initially wrote to him:

Dear Cousin Dorothy,

How wonderful! After these many, many years to have news of you and your father. We Brittons had lost sight of you and in spite of enquiries no trace of your father came to light. I did not know that your father had married. So it is indeed with pleasure that I shall look forward to meeting you. I remember your father going out to Japan very well, and I know he wrote to some of the home folk from time to time, and eventually all correspondence ceased. I can put you in touch with your father's half-brother's wife, who is still alive.

Take a taxi from the station, as I am nearly a mile from it. I am looking forward to our meeting <u>very much indeed.</u>

Like 'Uncle' George, Winifred, my father's half-sister-in-law, also welcomed me with open arms. She studied my face carefully, saying I did not look very Japanese. In the last letter they had received from Frank, at about the time of the First World War, he had said Japanese girls were so nice, we must not be surprised if he married one. Never hearing from him again, they had all surmised he had died in the Great Earthquake of 1923. She gave me a photo of her husband Cyril, my father's half-brother, as a young sailor on board a minesweeper during the First World War. She told me he often spoke of my father, who had sent him a Japanese bicycle when he was a boy.

Winifred was a lovely person. She sang in a choir, and was delighted to receive a copy of my cantata *And Certain Women Followed Him*, which had recently come out. She very sensibly commented that the title was too long, and would be better just called *And Certain*

Women. Not long after the thrill of discovering I had such a lovely aunt, Winifred died of cancer, and, tragically was soon followed by the death of her daughter, my newly-found first cousin Audrey, known as 'Betty'. I am still in touch with *her* daughter Elizabeth.

One of the Brittons *did* marry a Japanese girl! Uncle George's grandson Richard. Richard looked Boy and me up during his gap year at university. He wrote to me and said he was working his way around the world, and could I find some work he could do for a few months in Japan. My mother had made friends with the man in charge of room staff at the Marunouchi Hotel. He had retired from his job at the hotel and was running a small English language school and he said he would be very happy indeed if my cousin Richard Britton could teach some English conversation there. And Richard fell in love with Miyoko, a delightful Japanese girl who was also teaching there. They were married and are living happily in Hampstead, with their talented son Alexander, who is Information Technologist for the British Heart Foundation. I visit them whenever I am in England.

Moreover, 'Uncle' George informed me that his nephew – electrical engineer Charles Britton, OBE, son of his brother Sydney – was actually *in Japan* at that very moment with his second wife, representing English Electric! It was all getting more and more exciting. I could hardly wait to get back to Japan and tell my mother. But I had told Ikuma that I would not return to Japan until his wife had put her stamp on those divorce papers.

Ikuma had made me promise to fly back immediately he let me know that she had. On 12 March 1962, he sent a cable to me at the Drummonds' saying 'STAMPED COME BACK IMMEDIATELY = IKUMA', following it up with an ultra-passionate airmail letter. Thrilled, I flew back and we spent an ecstatic night together at a hotel. It turned out, however, that although his wife had reluctantly put her *hanko* (seal) on the papers, the divorce had not been finalized owing to complications having arisen over a certain Japanese cultural tradition. When divorcing in Japan it is customary for the wife to take back her maiden name. Kazuko refused to do so, and insisted on keeping Ikuma's surname in the Western way. In Japan it is traditionally a matter of the all-important family register. When divorced, the bride is expunged from it. So presumably in order to keep his surname, Kazuko would have had to legally change her surname to 'Dan', which worried Ikuma's family as to the various ways that might affect all of them in the future.

I had become pregnant. I decided on an abortion, since I was afraid the news, in those days, would kill my strait-laced mother, whom I could not bear to hurt. My wonderful German doctor, who had been in love with me since hearing my cantata – which had convinced him I was a reincarnation of Bach – tried to persuade me to go to England and secretly give birth there, and then go back later and adopt it. But I could not bear the thought of not being able to bond properly, straight away, with the child.

Mother was interested to hear of my finding all those Brittons, but strangely, she was hesitant about getting in touch with Norah and Charles. 'What if we don't like them?' she said. 'Oh Mother,' I said, 'they're Daddy's relatives! I don't care whether I'll like them or not. I want to meet them!'

Charles and Norah Britton could not have been nicer. And Mother was thrilled, too, because Charles not only looked very like my father, but was just fifty-four, the age Daddy was when he died. We became great friends, and when soon after we met them Charles was asked to be general manager of Hongkong Electric, they invited us there, to spend Christmas and New Year with them in their beautiful house on the Peak. They continued to invite us year, after year, and it became the high spot of our lives. Charles had been a rowing champion at university. I have a photo of him as a young man sitting beside a table covered with his rowing trophies. He was a sailing enthusiast too, and the first thing he did in Hong Kong was to have a big beautiful yacht built. Sailing amid the many islands there on the weekends during our visits was tremendous fun.

Norah was fascinated with my shell collection in Hayama and started a collection herself. Hong Kong was short of beaches, so whenever Charles had business in Tokyo she would come with him, and Norah and I would fly or take the bullet train to some part of Japan and hire a car and search the beaches. Together we covered a great deal of Japan's shores and found lots of shells.

CHAPTER 30

Sea Shells

✦

OKINAWA HAD NOT yet been returned to Japan by the American occupying forces, but Norah and I were eager to look for shells on the beaches of Ishigaki, an island at the far southern end of the Ryukyu archipelago, and so we had to get permission from SCAP. Norah and I agreed to meet at Naha, the capital of Okinawa. A celebrated marine zoologist from Australia, who was a pen friend of mine and had become a close friend, joined us there too.

Ishigaki was the nearest thing to heaven that I have ever encountered. Its beaches and bays were totally

unspoiled, in utterly unbelievable purity. I was cross
with Norah when we were having a picnic on one
of the beaches and she tossed a small can she had just
emptied into the prickly centre of a century plant.
'Oh, no-one will notice this one,' she said, as I pointed
out that the first one is just the way pollution begins.

The story of my friendship with Isobel Bennett is
a fascinating tale. A nice Australian couple from their
embassy that I got to know in Tokyo had rented a
house on the next beach, and I noticed a book they
had called *Australian Seashores* in which the shells and
creatures described sounded so similar to what we
find on the shore here in Hayama, that I asked if I
might borrow it for a few days. It was written by
William J. Dakin, professor emeritus of zoology at
the University of Sydney. At home, while studying
it at leisure, I suddenly came across a photograph that
reminded me of something I had seen years before,
as a child. At the time, no one I asked had any idea
what it might possibly be, and it was such a strange
creature, that over the years I had come to think that
it must be a figment of my imagination.

Beyond our house, there was a large rocky outcrop
that contained a hidden pool formed by rocks that
were white, while most of the other rocks, both there
and in front of our house, were shades of yellow and
grey. This little white pool with the sparkling clarity
of the water within it, always seemed special to me.
One day, I saw a truly fairy-like creature floating in it.
It was small and delicate, floating upside-down on its
back, with arms and legs stretched out with feathery

tips, its silvery blue skin patterned with dark blue lines. After gazing at it in wonder for some time, I lifted it out onto my hand. It did not move or try to get away, and while out of the water and on my hand it lost its featheryness, and became just a blob, head raised and looking like a miniature arctic seal. When I put it in my bucket with some water, it became a fairy again.

Coming across its photograph in Dakin's book, I was eager to find out more about my 'fairy', and decided I would write to the author, but according to the introduction, he had died just before the book came out, and so I wrote to his assistant, Isobel Bennett. She very kindly replied, saying she did not think I was a zoologist, but I was certainly very observant, and she said she would like to hear from me again and learn more about my Hayama seashore experiences.

We became pen friends, and she told me a great deal about the floating *glaucus,* and that I could expect to find them in quantity after a storm, together with lots of *janthina, physalia, velella* and *porpita,* which also float in the surface 'Blue Layer' of the sea, and on two of which the *glaucus* feeds. Their colour blue, she wrote, is for camouflage from predatory birds. In the book, the photograph of my *glaucus* was on the same page as several gaily coloured and patterned sea slugs, because they all belonged to the Nudibranch genus. Coincidentally, it was one of those sea slugs that I must have handed in a bucket to the policeman for Emperor Hirohito that day in the spring of 1934.

Isobel eventually came to Japan to attend a marine zoology congress, and spent a few days with me in Hayama. When I told Mr Kuroda, Emperor Hirohito's chamberlain, he arranged for her to have an audience with His Majesty. But when I asked a friend at the Australian Embassy whether they could provide a car to take her to the Palace, my friend said it would have to have been arranged from Canberra! So I took her myself in a taxi from the station, and we picked up Mr Kuroda at the Palace gate. I was allowed to ride with them as far as the Emperor's Study, known officially as The Biological Laboratory, Imperial Household, and Chamberlain Kuroda said he would take Isobel back afterwards to join me, if I waited at the Imperial Hotel. On my way back out of the Palace grounds I had to stop the taxi driver from speeding along the shady winding forested lanes of the Imperial gounds. Apologizing, he said it was because he was so excited, and when we emerged, he asked if he might park for a few moments to pull himself together. 'This marvellous experience is something for me to tell my children and grandchildren,' he said, as he wiped the sweat from his brow. When Isobel and I had first got into the taxi asking to be taken to the Palace, he had asked, 'Is it the pub on the Ginza you mean, or the Palace Baseball Stadium?'

In 1987, Isobel Bennett published a fully revised edition of W.J. Dakin's classic *Australian Seashores* with lots of superb coloured photographs taken by her. In it she refers to the *glaucus* as 'one of the most beautiful of all the sea creatures'.

Isobel Bennett became Australia's leading authority on Australian marine life, and also authored an authoritative book about the Great Barrier Reef. She received an honorary DSc, and was awarded the AO (Officer of the Order of Australia).

It was fascinating having Isobel with us on Ishigaki explaining so much of interest to us about the marine creatures we saw and collected. It was all so interesting we almost overstayed our visitor's permit. I had foolishly applied to SCAP for too little time. We had flown from Naha to Ishigaki in a Dakota, again foolishly on one-way tickets, and return flights on the small aircraft were all booked solid. Tadao Iwamoto, my favourite NHK producer, who was then based in Naha and had entertained us on our arrival, was worried when we failed to return to Naha, and got in touch with me to say he would have to get us on a ship. Cabins were not available, and we had to sleep in the communal lower deck sleeping space on mats laid together with dozens of passengers. The sea was somewhat rough, so we decided to try and get a bit of sleep outside, up on the deck. At Naha Mr Iwamoto and I saw Norah and Isobel off by air for Hong Kong and Sydney, respectively.

Our next Christmas and New Year in Hong Kong with Charles and Norah was our last, for my beloved mother died, after being bedridden for almost a year. It was 1966. I kept her company by working in her room on the Linguaphone Japanese course I had been asked to write. During that time, my cousin Gordon Daniels and his first wife, who had been spending several years in Kyoto and were just about to return to Sheffield, came to say goodbye, and there in her bedroom in reply to Gordon's question about it, Mother embarked for the last time on her usual spirited personal account of the 1923 earthquake. I have always remembered the story word for word from both my parents' accounts, as set down in the relevant chapter of this book.

Our housekeeper Kaneko-san became almost like a mother to me, and was a tremendous comfort after my mother died. She had been like a member of the family all along, looking after mother while I was away working. She even became fluent in Mother's hilarious pidjin Japanese, which Mother had picked up from her Yokohama friends. It had been called the 'Yokohama Dialect' in a humorous book by that name written by an early Bluff resident. For instance, boiling water was called *sampo mizu* (walking water) and once when Mother told me Kaneko-san had seen lots of shooting stars, I couldn't believe Mother would know the Japanese for shooting stars, and Kaneko-san told me Mother had called them '*otsukisama chigaimas pokan*' (those things not-the-moon going wham). *Pokan* is the sound a thing makes when you throw it down, and Mother had heard my nanny years ago telling me not to throw my toys onto the floor!

Charles and Norah came to Mother's funeral. Very soon afterwards Charles retired. He had designed their yacht for comfort, thinking they could possibly sail it home to England on Charles's retirement, and live in it, moored in one of England's beautiful rivers. But by the time he retired, Charles no longer felt quite up to boat life without the helping hand of the Hong Kong Yacht Club's Chinese boat-boy. They sold it and settled on Alderney, one of Britain's Channel Islands, where Boy (and Derek) and I visited them after we were married.

CHAPTER 31

The 'Katakana Prison' and Mr Suzuki

✦

HAVING LEARNED HOW to speak Japanese that sounds like Japanese, and French that sounds like French, one of my fondest wishes has always been to help Japanese people speak English that sounds like English, and escape from what I call their 'katakana prison'. But the only private lessons I have had time to give was to Yukiko, the daughter of my best friend Wakako. Yukiko eventually became chief of our Hayama town council! I also helped Mr Shimura with his small English conversation school in Kamakura. He is the teacher I mentioned who used to say *kana hiki eigo wa kanashiki eigo* (English in kana is pathetic English). He spoke beautiful English because his father had sent him to study in England. He used to tell a very amusing story about a happening on his way to England by ship. He made friends with an Australian girl whose mother was in bed seasick for the first few days. Next time he met the girl he asked how her mother was. She replied, 'Mother is coming up on deck to die,' and Shimura-san was very worried not knowing the correct way to act at someone's funeral on a deck at sea. But it was only her Australian pronunciation. What she had said was that her mother was 'coming up on deck today!' So when he got to England he made sure he learned how to speak English that sounded English, and not Australian!

Copying one's native speaker teacher's useful phrases over and over and over again until one gets them sounding exactly the same, just like I started French, is what I believe is the very best way to learn English. I stressed that method in a book published in 1976 entitled *Dorothy obasan no johin na eikaiwa* (Auntie Dorothy's Fine English Conversation), which did not sell well because buyers were put off by the word *johin* which also means 'refined'! Another publisher brought out my next one, which they called *Eikaiwa omoshiro seminaa* (Lively English Seminar) that did far better!

My books elicited a phone call from a lady who said she and her husband had started a school teaching children English in a similar way, using what they called the 'Direct Method' based on the exclusive use of native speakers as teachers. I became Adviser to Mr & Mrs Kyokuta's school, which was called Matty's, and was chief judge at their annual speech contests. After nearly forty years, Matty's has now been taken over by Katsuko Okabe, the British-educated daughter of my Danish flutist neighbour, who calls it Katty's. I believe the 'Direct Method' is sometimes also called the 'Natural Method'. But I was soon to discover the ultimate method of them all, for learning almost everything from music to language: Shin'ichi Suzuki's 'Mother Tongue Method' for learning the violin!

On one of my weekly NHK Radio Japan programmes I used to interview prominent members of the Japanese music world. One of them was violinist, educator, philosopher and humanitarian Shin'ichi Suzuki, founder of Talent Education, whose revolutionary 'mother tongue' approach for teaching small children the violin is now world famous. He was the son of a man who had founded the largest violin factory in the world. I went to his home and violin school in the castle town of Matsumoto, close to the Japan Alps, and was staggered to see little boys and girls with tiny violins following him around the room playing Bach and Vivaldi with the style and tone of professional musicians. And, moreover, enjoying it so much, just as if they were playing a game! No exercises, no scales, no printed music, just imitating their teacher, playing beautiful music and looking and sounding like him. Suzuki did, in fact, often make it like a game. While they played their violins as they walked, he would sometimes ask them simple questions, like, 'How many legs have you?' and they would joyfully shout 'two!' without missing a beat. He tried to make their violin playing second nature, like speech. His teaching was successful because it was done with love, wanting to make the children happy.

Suzuki always stressed the fact that his method was based on the way children learned to speak their mother tongue. I was fascinated, because *that* is exactly the way I had learned Japanese, from my nanny, and how I began French, with the French nun. I was green with envy. If only I could have learned the violin that way too!

Suzuki was in his thirties when the thought first occurred to him how children learn to speak fluent Japanese. He was teaching violin at the Imperial Conservatory at the time, and a man had brought his four-year-old son and asked Suzuki to teach him. Completely flummoxed at the idea of teaching such a small child how to play the violin, and wondering how on earth to go about it, the thought had suddenly struck him. The little boy, Suzuki's first Talent Education pupil, was Toshiya Eto who went on to become world-famous, as so many of his pupils have done. Suzuki believed that musical ability is not an inborn talent but something which can be developed by any child, just as all Japanese children learn to speak Japanese. He maintained that a child's potential is unlimited. Suzuki's method, was a revelation to me, and proved that how I had learned both Japanese and French, was just the way foreign languages ought to be taught! Surprisingly, teaching music was not Suzuki's main purpose. He writes that he just wanted to make 'good citizens, noble human beings'!

When Mr Suzuki's German wife Waltraud asked me if I would correct her efforts as she strove to translate into English Suzuki's book entitled *Ai ni ikiru: sainou wa umaretsuki de nai* (Fostered by Love: talent is not inborn) (Kodansha, Tokyo, 1966) I was so impressed by Suzuki's method that I wanted the whole world to read his inspiring book as soon as possible, so I offered to translate it myself straight away from his Japanese, while allowing Waltraud to take the credit as her husband fervently desired. They were very grateful, and in return, they planted a beautiful *saru-suberi*, a crape myrtle tree, in the school's garden in Matsumoto with my name on it! The English translation was published in 1969 by Exposition Press, New York, entitled *Nurtured by Love: A New Approach to Education*.

In it, Suzuki describes how he insists the infants begin with Mozart's Variations on the French song *Ah vous dirai-je, maman* which English speakers know as 'Twinkle Twinkle Little Star'. First of all he teaches the child's mother to play the melody, and gives them a recording to play at home, and before long, the child becomes eager to have a go. And after they have finally memorized the music, he says, 'Now we will practise playing it beautifully!'

I believe some of the Talent Education schools now use the method in teaching piano, cello and flute in addition to violin. But I wonder if they have realized it is the ideal way of learning foreign languages too. It is so simple and so effective. Just based on imitation. Imitating one's native-speaker teacher, or even phrases on a CD, over and over and over again, until one gets the sounds and rhythm right! Learning a song is an excellent way to begin, because the rhythm is already there. Of course that is not the end. You have to develop your vocabulary and grammatical phraseology. But you have observed the invaluable first step. Like Suzuki's little violinists, you have got onto the right train, and you are well on the way.

How truly wonderful it would be if more and more Japanese people could break out of their 'katakana prison' and speak English that SOUNDS like English, and thereby interact better with the world!

CHAPTER 32

Poetry

✦

ANOTHER JOB I used to have at NHK was translating into English examples of their TV and radio programmes that they entered in international competitions. The competition always required printed translations, in one or two languages, of the programme, for the judges. One of the many programme entries that I translated was a popular radio programme, one of a regular series by a famous authority on the *Man'yoshu*, the world's earliest anthology of poems, dating back to the eighth century, written by members of all sections of the Japanese populace from royalty to commoners. Most of the poems are five-line tanka, which combine a haiku-like triplet (three lines of 5, 7, and 5 syllables) and a couplet (two lines of 7 syllables each).

The several poems in that programme NHK were submitting were not only quite remarkable, but Professor Takashi Inukai's talks about them were so good that I was utterly enthralled, and became a member of his fan club, which included many celebrities. At several of the club meetings I sang with my Irish harp some of my compositions of *Man'yoshu* poems that I had set to music, singing them in both Japanese and my English translations. My favourite was this fascinating pair of poems entitled *The Mountain Dew* – a prince's poetic complaint for having waited so long for his date, and his date's reply.

Prince Ohtsu wrote:

On yon hillside steep,
Waiting there for you my love,
Waiting, oh, so long,
My raiment was drenchéd through,
Wet with drops of mountain dew!

Lady Ishikawa's reply:

Waiting there for me,
My lord was all drenchéd through;
How I envy you
O lucky dew! How I wish
I had been that mountain dew!

I had written poetry since I was quite small, inspired
by the many books of verse given to me by my parents
and overseas relatives, all of which I loved. I did not
come across Japanese haiku and tanka until I returned
to Japan after the war. In my father's bookcase I
was fascinated to find an enormous volume called
An Anthology of Haiku Ancient and Modern translated
and annotated by Asataro Miyamoto and published
by Maruzen in 1932. A few translations by early
Western scholars are even included. That is when
I discovered how the Japanese make the readers of
poems and the gazers at paintings do part of the work.
While Western paintings and poetry tend to describe
things clearly and fully, in Japan, much of the subject
is merely suggested, and the reader and gazer must
complete the oeuvre in their minds. The author in
the Introduction explains that the book is the result
of Prince Takamatsu, Emperor Hirohito's brother,
having asked to be lectured by him on the subject
of the translation by Western scholars of Japanese
literature, as well as aspects of Anglo-Japanese translation in general, and that the Prince had contributed
generously to the publication of the book.

One remarkable thing about Japan, as Lafcadio
Hearn is said to have observed, everyone in this
country is a poet. From time immemorial they have
been led in this by the Imperial Family, who still start
the year with an annual Poetry Reading at the Palace.
Each year a subject is set, and tanka by the members of
the Imperial Family, beginning with the Emperor, are
read out by an official reader, after which a selected

few from those sent in by commoners from both Japan and abroad are also read.

The haiku form now seems to have become internationally popular. I have never felt a desire to compose haiku or tanka myself, preferring to describe my poetic feelings uninhibitedly, as we do in the West, but I do love the exciting challenge of trying to translate tanka and haiku effectively into English. Many are those who try. A book by New York-based poet and commentator Hiroaki Sato was published in 1986 called *One Hundred Frogs,* with that number of English versions of Basho's most famous haiku! Mine is among them:

> Listen! A frog
> Jumping into the stillness
> Of an ancient pond.

Some years ago a wonderful man called Saburo Nobuki was on a regular TV discussion programme with me, and we often met for lunch beforehand at a nearby restaurant. He kept asking my opinion about books and translating and such like, and if I had any writing plans. I said I was eager to publish my poems and wondered if he could suggest a publisher. He wisely advised me first to get as many published as possible separately in magazines. He did not tell me then, but I think he must have been sounding me out, because fairly soon after that he became Director of the newly established Kodansha International, a branch of Japan's premier publisher

Kodansha. He asked me to translate Ryunosuke Akutagawa's fascinating retelling of *Tu Tze-chun,* an old
Chinese legend, which they published in a stunning
edition with woodcuts by Naoko Matsubara. Soon
afterwards K.I. asked me to do a new translation of
haiku master Basho's classic *Oku no hosomichi* (The
Narrow Road to a Far Province). They published it
under the title *A Haiku Journey,* for it describes the
poet's longest poetic pilgrimage.

A little way along in his masterpiece Basho writes:

> It was not until we finally reached the checkpoint,
> or barrier, at Shirakawa that we felt we were really
> on our way at last.

A few years ago, to mark the hundredth anniversary
of world Rotary, its local Japanese branch set up a
splendid statue of Basho at New Shirakawa railway
station, with those words on the plinth in my English
translation as well as Basho's Japanese original.

I began my Introduction to *A Haiku Journey* with
the first stanza of my poem entitled 'A Seashell'. That
opening stanza is the nearest thing to a haiku or tanka
that I have written. It is actually a long poem and has
five stanzas, which could be said to summarize my
life rather well:

> A sea shell
> Is a Japanese poem
> Of seventeen syllables
> Small and formal in shape

But containing an ocean
Of thoughts

Love in sea-girt places
Windswept
Or still enough to smell
The faint warm scent of palmetto

A native girl
Remembers that fabulous hill shape
Floating over the sea
And how the sea
Was her lover
Long ago in the fanciful years

And now the sea
Is a murmuring around the feet
Of a man and a woman
Hands-clasped weaving dreams
Into the sound
Of its unfathomable waves

The dancing heart
The tears
All this is told
In the shape of a shell

Saburo Nobuki used to brag he had discovered me
as a translator, and when he retired from Kodansha
International he published a magazine in Japanese
called *Japan Avenue,* for which he invited me write

a regular piece called *Hayama no Nikki* (Hayama Diary), bragging he had now discovered an essayist – whose 'skill' had been honed for me by the editors of a popular daily column in the *Asahi Shinbun* called *sutendo gurasu* (Stained Glass)! It had continued for three years at the time of the 1964 Tokyo Olympics. It started off with seven writers – one for each day – four of us foreigners who were required to write in English which would be translated; but I had insisted on writing in Japanese, and their editing of my attempts were a marvellous course of instruction for me!

CHAPTER 33

The Island in Between

✦

As TIME WENT on, I found myself writing and translating more and more and composing less and less. Looking back, I think God must have gently been arranging for me to see less and less of Ikuma, and getting Ikuma back to his wife and son. Ikuma had obviously become very fond of the intriguing-sounding little boy, nicknamed 'Choko-chan' because of the way he toddled about choko-choko, full of curiosity. Ikuma spoke of him to me so often. God, whom I believe is the almighty power of Nature, began by setting a beautiful island between us. Ikuma had been persuaded by his musical hero, Kosçak Yamada (1886–1965), the doyen of Japanese Western-style music composers, to build a holiday villa on Hachijo Island, the furthest away from Hayama in the long Izu Islands chain, perfect for fishing, which was Ikuma's hobby. Ikuma built his house on the plot next to Yamada's, which is still empty. 'When are you coming to see it?' Ikuma would constantly ask me, adding, 'You will like it there. I've even provided a special desk for you to work on.' But a house on a wooded mountain high up from the sea did not appeal to me at all, for I am a beach person, so I never went.

Besides spending more and more time on Hachijo Island, Ikuma was also spending more and more time in China. He died there on his sixty-seventh visit. Kazuko had died the year before in Japan. As a Japanese who had mastered the fundamentals of Western music, Ikuma Dan had a special feeling for that land, with its early connections with Western civilisation via the Silk Road. Ikuma had even composed a beautiful symphony with that name. His opera Yuzuru was performed in Peking in 1979, the first ever work by a foreign composer, and Dan was warmly welcomed by their leading composers whom he found to be congenial companions to chat with about music's origins and trends.

Yuzuru, truly a masterpiece, has been performed in Japan over 700 times, and I have always wondered why his other fascinating operas - which I translated - have not had the same success. But it appears that

Japan's music critics and media have gone overboard in praising young composers who superficially try to be fashionably avant garde, whereas Ikuma's music was adequately modern without discarding its traditional heart. Like Ikuma, I hate music that is dissonant just for the sake of modernity, but I like experimenting with sounds that are expressive in all sorts of new ways. I shall never forget our remarkable compatibility, and I do so wish we could have gone on collaborating. And I shall never forget the beautiful letters he wrote expressing his love for me.

After Boy left Japan towards the end of the Korean War, he too wrote me many, many very beautiful letters recalling all the details of the happiness of his time in Hayama with me – finding shells and sea horses on the beach, planting the sago palm we had found that had been thrown out by one of the summer beach huts, which we lugged home and planted at the bottom of our steps. Boy used to say that if it thrived, so would our love. Before he left he had made me promise that if I fell I love with anyone else I would let him know, so I was a good girl and wrote and told him when I fell in love with Ikuma. And when I left for England on the boat with the elephants Ikuma made me promise I would not see Boy. So I did not try to do so. But I had not promised I would not phone him, and I could not resist the temptation just to hear his voice. I intended to hang up if his wife or sister-in-law answered the phone. Boy answered, asked for my number and then called me back from a nearby phone box. Derek was with him, he said.

Boy badly wanted to meet me, and when I told him I had promised not to see him, he wept. Later, he wrote to me saying how sad he had been not to see me, and begged me never to come to England again without somehow arranging a meeting.

Ikuma had become friends with Crown Prince Akihito and Princess Michiko after composing a beautiful grand march for wind orchestra entitled Celebration at the time of their marriage in 1959. In addition, Ikuma's wife Kazuko, had become an excellent cook, having had lessons with Mr Kaneko, the husband of our housekeeper, and they used often to invite the royals to dinner when they came to Hayama. By that time, Ikuma and Kazuko and little son lived in a new house high up on a hill in Kuruwa, a short way down the peninsula from Hayama.

The last time Ikuma and I were together was an extraordinarily happy occasion when we had dinner with the Emperor and Empress at the Hayama Villa. Their Majesties had invited me together with Ikuma and Kazuko. Their Majesties seemed delighted to hear that Ikuma and I had been childhood friends, and Ikuma's usual lively conversation made it a thoroughly delightful evening. I shall always think of that dinner as a very, very beautiful ending to my relationship with Ikuma. God was working for us both.

CHAPTER 34

Marrying 'Boy' – 1968

✦

BOY WROTE THAT his wife had died, that he still loved me very much, and still considered his days in Hayama as the happiest in his life. I said 'yes' to his next letter proposing marriage. But then almost immediately he wrote to me saying a good friend had told him that he had no right to saddle a young woman with his incapacitated son Derek, and that he had sorrowfully come to the conclusion the friend was right. But God had already intervened! The manager of the Yomiuri Symphony had just rung me up and asked if I had any need to go to England, because they could give me a one-way ticket if I would meet English-horn player Barry Tuckwell in London and try to persuade him to come to Tokyo as a guest for a short period. I had accepted the Symphony's offer. It worked out well for me because it was just at the beginning of the August Japanese school holiday, when I would not have to go to NHK for the fortnightly recordings of my weekly Junior High English Classroom TV programme. So after writing letters backwards and forwards, Boy and I agreed I should go and stay with them in his flat and see Derek for myself.

Boy told me to take a train from London to Brighton, which was fairly close to Worthing, where he lived, and had hourly trains, which Worthing did not. I asked in the station where people from outside usually come in, and I stationed myself in a good place to see Boy as soon as he arrived. The first man I saw was old and grey, bent over and using a stick. Oh dear, I thought. After all it was fourteen years since I last saw Boy and he was twenty-six years older than I was. But it was not he! The next man was in a wheelchair. And thank goodness that was not Boy either. There were horse races on apparently, and traffic was congested, so he was delayed. When he finally did appear, I was happy to see that he seemed as sprightly as ever. He had left Derek at the house of his friend Clare, where we picked him up and started for Boy's home. Derek is a 'back-seat driver' and gets upset if you do not drive in the direction he thinks you should. He shows his displeasure by hissing and clapping. Boy never liked criticism, and turned around and shouted at him. I was quite surprised! But peace took over as we neared their garden, brimming over with gorgeous roses of various colours and other flowering bushes. Like many British people, Boy was an enthusiastic, indefatigable and enterprising gardener.

Boy and I were thrilled to be together again. And I loved Derek with his laughter and his smile. He was just my sort of person. I love to see people smile. I have always strongly considered that a smile makes every woman beautiful and every man handsome! I once even gave a talk on that theme to a graduating class of girls at the St Maur International School in Yokohama.

While spending that month of August in Worthing, Boy and Derek and I had happy strolls together along 'the front' as it was known – the avenue beside the sea with a wide, raised pavement between the road and the pebbly beach. Many people retired to Worthing, Brighton and other towns on the southern coast because it was a little sunnier than most of England. As we strolled along we would often see cars draw up beside the pavement and an elderly couple would get out for a breath of sea air, and Derek would stop walking and watch them get out of their car, and if they were old and rheumatic, he would follow their painful movements saying 'uuh' and 'ooh.' They seldom looked pleased, but Derek was following their movements with compassion! He follows conversation closely too that way. If one is talking about something happy, his face is filled with joy, but if the subject is sad, so is he.

Boy had moved to the flat on the sea front in Worthing because its view of the English Channel reminded him of our view of the sea in Hayama, which he had liked so much. It was originally a two-storey house which had been made into two flats just before Boy and his family moved in. His unmarried sister-in-law lived with them and did the cooking. She had died fairly soon after his wife. Clare, at whose house Boy had left Derek while he came to fetch me, owned the downstairs flat as well as her house. She was a widow, and had her eye on Boy, as also several other widows in Worthing did. He was considered quite a prize with his good looks and his knighthood, which would make any woman marrying him a Lady! To make it seem proper for a youngish woman to be staying in his flat, he had told his friends I was an *au pair* (a young foreign person helping with house-work)! The neighbours apparently referred to me as 'that Korean girl' because of Boy's connection with the Korean War! When Clare heard he was going to marry me, she tried hard to persuade him to marry *her* instead, because she was his age, and she told him she thought I was far too young for him, and it would not work out. But after failing to persuade him, she very kindly gave us a lovely little wedding recep-tion in the garden of her house after our marriage on 14 August at the town's Registry. We flew back to Japan soon afterwards because I had to get back for my TV programme. My producer was at the airport to welcome us, having read about our marriage in the Japanese newspaper.

The 'Nice Guest' as she always used to call Boy, received a very warm welcome in Hayama by my wonderful housekeeper Kaneko-san, but a frightening scene ensued when we went upstairs. Boy and I were to have my mother's room, and Derek the little room next to it, which was mine in the days when Boy used to visit us. All of a sudden, Boy shouted angrily, 'Who painted that picture of you?'

It was hanging on the wall behind the bed in the room that used to be mine and was now to be Derek's. The painting was not of me. It was a beautiful oil painting of the back of a naked woman lying on a beach facing out to sea towards which a man's departing foot prints could be seen in the sand. It had been painted by a friend, who gave it to me because I had admired it. I liked it because it made me think of Boy leaving me in Hayama when he went off home to England. Boy refused to believe me, and the fact that my friend had writtten on the back in French: 'A la Duchésse de Hayama' did not help. Boy swore it was a painting of me, and I got the feeling he wanted to throw me over then and there and go back to the UK and have nothing more to do with me. I was distraught. I just did not know what to do. I was desperate. 'All right, I'll burn it,' I said, and rushed down onto the beach straight away and did so. Boy simply refused to believe me, no matter how hard I tried to explain that it had not been painted of me.

Three young men from Switzerland working for the Red Cross Society just after the Korean War had been introduced to me by their boss, the SCAP Red

Cross representative, an American lady who had lived in Japan before the war and was an old friend of my mother's. All three of them were gaye, and they had rented a house in Hayama. Their job was to travel to Sado Island off Japan's western coast each time a ship set off from there for Korea. They interviewed those Korean residents of Japan who wanted to return to their homeland, to find out which Korea they really wanted to go to, and make sure their desire was genuine and that they were not being coerced. One of the young men was an artist, and it was he who gave me that painting.

After that disturbing beginning blew over, Boy and Derek and I were immensely happy in Hayama. Boy used to say he did not think Derek had ever been so happy. We even found a sea-horse on the shoreline, the first time we three went down onto the beach. It was the first sea-horse I had found since Boy left, and was a joyous omen. Boy had mentioned them so much in his letters. Boy, Derek and I were so happy in Hayama that we often had triple 'hug-ins'. Derek loved walking along the beach with us and bathing in the sea. I tried to teach him to swim, but it was impossible because he could not relax enough to float. So the best I could do was just hold him while he enjoyed kicking his legs. One of our first Christmas cards had a photograph of us sitting on the beach in bathing costumes, and Alice Morland wrote that we all three looked exactly the same age! We bought two bicycles, one for Derek and one for me so Derek and I could bicycle together all around the still empty roads of a large nearby fill-in before it became built over. Derek had not cycled for years, but had not forgotten how. Boy told me Derek had taught himself to ride on the maid's bicycle when they lived at Cowley Cottage, a centuries-old house in Uxbridge, with extensive grounds interspersed with little lanes.

During the Korean War, Boy had become friends with Admiral Arleigh '21 knots' Burke whom he always sat next to at General MacArthur's briefings. Burke went on to become Chief of Naval Operations for an unprecedented six years, and is considered to be the father of the modern US Navy. When he heard that Boy had married me and would be living in Hayama, he made us members of the US Naval Base in Yokosuka. There we became very close friends with Admiral Julian Burke and his wife. Julian, no relation to Arleigh, was Commander US Naval Forces Japan. We saw a great deal of them.

Boy and I often played golf at the US Air Force base at Atsugi, which was not too far away, and Derek used to greatly enjoy pushing our golf cart. And many happy evenings were spent playing bridge with our delightful German neighbours Roland and Erna Sonderhoff. I was an eager beginner in both games!

My TV programme to schools started again almost as soon as we three arrived in Japan. Leaving Derek with wonderful Kaneko-san, Boy came with me to my fortnightly recording sessions at NHK. He insisted on going there with me every time. I greatly enjoyed having his company on the hour-long train journey and the longer drive home in the NHK car, but I think his main reason for coming was because he did not trust me alone at NHK, where he was afraid I might run into Ikuma. Every time the phone rang he would come and watch me as I answered it.

I feel I am such an honest and trustworthy person, who would never dream of carrying on an affair behind someone's back, that I began to resent Boy's lack of trust in me. I even prayed to God to *cure* my resentment. But I realize now that *I* was not *doing* what God had told me to do through the words of Jesus and Saint Paul: to just 'put on love'! And how does one go about putting on love? I should have first put on humbleness, meekly acknowledging any possible offence on my part, and then I should have wiped what must have been an unpleasant look of resentment off my face and just smiled lovingly, even if I did not feel like smiling, and I should have tried to hug him, even if he pushed me away. I should have just loved him as hard as I could. Mother Teresa has said 'love until it hurts!' Paul wrote:

> Put off all these: anger, wrath and malice. Put off all these; Put off the old man with his deeds. And put on the new man that is after the image of Him that created him; where there is neither Greek, nor Jew, Barbarian, Scythian, bond nor free, and Christ is all in all. Put on, therefore, bowels of mercies, kindness, humbleness, meekness, long suffering; forbearing one another and forgiving one another, even as Christ forgave you. And above all these things, put on love, which is the bond of perfectness!

Those words, from Paul's letter to the Colossians, sums up Christianity for me, and I set them to music in my song entitled *Put on Love*. While soloist for several years at the Christian Science Association's church services at the US Naval Base in Yokosuka, not far from Hayama, I found there was a dearth of songs that I felt were effective, so I composed about a dozen with words from the Bible. My first, *Know Ye that the Lord He is God*, was published by the Boston Music Company, and is still sung in various churches in the UK and USA. The Boston Music Company had signed a contract with me to publish half a dozen more of my sacred songs, but did not immediately bring the others out, because they said the market for sacred songs was poor, so I cancelled the contract, thinking to try in the UK, but I became so busy I never did anything more about it!

I had also wanted very much to compose another cantata, which I was going to call *One*, expressing my feeling that all the religions of the world are basically the same – Shinto, with its *Amaterasu O-mikami* (Great Goddess who Illuminates the Heavens); Islam with its Allah is Great; Buddhism's compassion towards all living beings – and that they should all stop fighting one another as they do, even within the same religions! I am not a churchgoer. I just want to try and follow Jesus and Paul's wonderful injunctions which are so challenging. All much more difficult than just going to church. It is possibly the most difficult thing in the world to '...love your enemies, bless them

that curse you, do good to them that hate you, and
pray for them which spitefully use you, and persecute
you'. But that is just what Jesus tells us to do! (see
Matthew 5:44).

I also love singing praises to God. I even once
thought how nice it would be to obtain an unused
church where sacred songs could be set out ready
for people who are able to read music to just go in
and sing them at specified times when an organist
would be ready. Each time I visit England I see more
and more disused churches, and they make me wish
I were younger! No sermons. Nothing else. Just
praising God in song! To my mind, God is Nature –
the almighty power causing all the phenomena of the
physical world. He is everywhere. As Tennyson said,
'Closer is He than breathing, and nearer than hands
and feet!' He is all the sciences – biology, evolution,
natural selection and all the rest, for God is all in all.
Christian Science defines God so well as Truth, Life,
Love, Mind, Spirit, Soul, Principle. I think of Him
especially as Life and Love!

A friend once told me he left his wife because
she did not make him feel good about himself.
I wish my mother had known more about men,
and had told me how sensitive they are. And that
they are particularly sensitive about their sexual
performance, which, as Marylin Monroe pointed
out does not matter all that much to women. Once
I even seriously contemplated suicide, so distraught
was I at unknowingly having hurt that sensitivity
in Boy. We were having a delightful time on an

eight-passenger merchant ship taking a short trip
back to England after our marriage, when one evening during coffee and liqueurs for all eight of us in
the Captain's suite, I was fascinated by a valuable
book the skipper had, and asked if I could borrow
it, promising I would return it in the morning.
Back in our cabin Boy angrily spat out the words:
'They'll all think you've got nothing else to do at
night but read that book' and he hid his face in
the bedclothes and would not speak to me. I ran
outside, wanting to throw myself overboard, and
paced the deck, in despair. Fortunately, the thought
of Derek finally prevented me from jumping into
the ocean.

That blew over too, thank goodness, and we
enjoyed the rest of the journey to London, this
time going through the Panama Canal – the very
first time for both of us. We had to cut our time
in London short in order to return by ship, having
been hastily notified of a sudden decision by the firm
to sell its ships. We caught the last one back. Boy
always wanted to avoid flying since he feared his
long luck in the air might be running out! And then
finally, after only ten happy years in Hayama we
moved back to Worthing, because Boy was having
trouble with his heart, and wanted to be near doctors who spoke English. I told him how good the
doctors now were in Japan, and the excellent hospitals, and urged him to stay, saying the language
would be no problem since he had me to interpret
for him. But there again was his lack of trust in me.

He said, 'How would I ever know whether you had translated truthfully?'

We were not very happy in Worthing. He himself kept admitting how happy we had been in Hayama, and I think he chided himself for having made the wrong decision, which made him even more unhappy. He was always hard on himself that way. He was even miserable when he lost at chess with me. Cross with himself for not having played better. And he was hard on his body, too. He would not let me drive, and insisted on walking along the cold, windy seafront when we were invited to friends' houses, without putting on a really properly warm coat. I am sure this did him no good at all, and brought on the heart attack that did him in.

Boy died on 19 June 1979. At the beautiful September memorial service in St Clement Danes, the RAF church for which Boy had collected the money to rebuild, I was very moved indeed when they told me that the bell ringers had insisted on taking part so they could ring a special chime for him, since one of the bells bore his name 'Boy'.

And who should appear among the mourners but Ted Hall. He was back from the Gold Coast, which was now independent and called Ghana. He was Protocol Officer at the Foreign and Commonwealh Office, with an MVO (Member of the Royal Victorian Order) he used to say he got for his advice to the Royal Family on how to seat their guests! He had read Boy's obituary in the *Daily Telegraph*. He came to see me afterwards in our flat in Worthing, and I was very touched by his reaction to Derek. 'I think he's rather sweet,' he said. We enjoyed Ted's company quite a few times in Worthing, and when I decided that autumn to sell the flat and return to Japan, where plenty of work awaited me, Ted was just about to retire from the Foreign and Commonealth Office, and told me he had spent so much of his life abroad, that he had few friends in Preston, Lancashire, where his home was, and he planned to sell his house there and spend his life travelling and visiting friends abroad. He asked if he could begin by visiting me in Hayama. He got along so well with Derek that I said he would be welcome in Hayama any time.

CHAPTER 35

The Japanese Crane –
Bird of Happiness

✦

IN 1980, WIDOWED and back in Japan, I had a
telephone call from my publishers Kodansha International asking me if I was interested at all in cranes.
I thought about it for a moment and said, 'Yes, I have
loved them since I was a small child'.

When we were living in Hayama soon after the
Great Earthquake, my mother and I often walked
down a long narrow lane to the beach. It divided two
properties: on the right was the beautiful garden and
summer villa of Prince Takamatsu, second brother

of Hirohito, who had become emperor on the death of their father, the Taisho emperor, who had just recently died in the Imperial Villa Annex, which was on the left of the lane. A high black wooden fence enclosed that shady pine-wooded property, which had afterwards been given over for his use to Prince Mikasa, the youngest of the imperial brothers. He had not yet received the title Mikasa, and was known then as Sumi no Miya, the Prince of Sumi. Sumi was written with a lovely kanji character meaning clear, lucid, limpid and serene, but to my young mind, sumi meant 'charcoal', which is written with a different kanji, but is pronounced the same way. So I always thought of him as Prince Charcoal, because I was sure that was why his fence was charcoal black.

And in that charcoal-coloured fence there happened to be a knot hole just at my eye-level, and when I peeked in, what should I see but a family of cranes! A father and mother and baby crane. I knew what they were, because my art-loving mother had reproductions of cranes by famous Japanese wood-block print artists. These were bronze sculptures, very life-like, but I had no reason to think they were not living cranes, although they *were* rather quiet. I always looked for them every time my mother or my nanny took me down that lane to the beach.

And all through the war years that my mother and I spent in Bermuda, my mother had with her a silk *furoshiki* – one of those lovely Japanese traditional gift-wrapping squares – with a beautiful painting of cranes on it, which we had hanging on the wall of our entrance hall. So cranes had continued to be my companions.

When Kodansha International asked me to write a book about the Japanese crane, I was thrilled. Moreover, to write a book about the crane seemed to me a perfect tribute to the memory of my beloved aeroplane pilot husband, who had died only the year before. While living in Japan, we had greatly enjoyed watching programmes together about Japanese cranes on television, for Boy loved birds, and so often used to say, 'I was a bird once'. Much later, when I was editing his autobiography, *Spitfires in Japan,* I was even tempted to use that phrase of his for the book's title!

Kodansha International sent me by air to Kushiro. It was the first time I had been to the eastern part of Japan's northernmost island. Hokkaido has an atmosphere all its own, quite unlike the rest of Japan. Because the Japanese had a natural aversion to cold-weather living, Hokkaido was left to Japan's aboriginal Ainu after they had been driven up there in the early centuries. It was not really settled by the Japanese people proper until late in the nineteenth century, when dairy farming, the raising of cattle, sheep, and pigs, and the cultivation of such things as potatoes, apples and hops was begun on American patterns. The wide open plateaus and gently rolling hills lend themselves to this kind of agriculture much better than to the rice cultivation of Japan's other islands with their abrupt hills and little flat-bottomed valleys. With its elms and poplars and ranches, and dotted about with silos and American-style buildings with mansard roofs, crossing the straits from Honshu to Hokkaido is almost like going to a foreign land.

Tsuneo Hayashida, Japan's leading crane photographer – whose beautiful photograph of a crane used to decorate Japan's thousand yen bank note – met me at Kushiro airport and drove me all around the large area of the seventy-five thousand acre Kushiro Marsh, the crane's main habitat, which is now a National Park. Marshes are ideal nesting places for cranes, as the reedy vegetation grows tall and thick, hiding nests from view, and the soft, wet nature of the land makes it virtually inaccessible to man and beast alike. Streams meander in and out, and it is on sandbars in river shallows that cranes sleep, standing up on one leg, and not in trees like most birds do.

Mr Hayashida took me to Tsuruimura, ('the village where cranes are') where we watched about forty birds pecking in the snow for grains of corn scattered for them by a farmer's wife, and we also visited the Crane Observation Centre at nearby Akan. Before flying to Kushiro, I had never seen a live crane. Nor have most Japanese people, but just as it was with me, the bird has always seemed very real to them because they are such an icon, and they appear on so many things, including wedding kimonos, saké bottles, and aeroplanes, and are considered tokens of good fortune, marital fidelity, longevity and such like. I called my book *The Japanese Crane, Bird of Happiness*. Falling in love with these graceful ballerinas nearly as tall as I am, I decided to donate my royalties towards their preservation. And during one of my visits to Kushiro I met young George Archibald whose marvellous International Crane Foundation had just started up in Barraboo, Wisconsin. Hopefully it will ensure the survival of all fifteen types species of the remarkable bird.

Strangely, back in Hayama, the very day I started work on the book, what should I find on the beach but a scrap of blue-and-white Edo-period porcelain with a crane on it! I have only found two fragments with cranes on them, and I found the second one, believe it or not, on the day I finished work on the book!

CHAPTER 36

Comfort and Solace with Ted

✦

WHEN DEREK AND I left London on 6 October 1979, one month after Boy's memorial service, Ted drove Derek and me to Heathrow, where he proposed to me. I had always liked Ted immensely, ever since we met again at the BBC, but I was never in love with him. We corresponded during the time he was in Ghana until he received my marriage announcement. He was not a flirtatious person at all so his letters were interesting, but unemotional, with no amorous insinuations in them at all, in spite of that hurried farewell hand press in the BBC canteen. When I once told

Ted that someone had said I was the most Christian person they had ever met, Ted replied that I was the most *reasonable* person *he* had ever known! Perhaps that was what appealed to him about me, as well as my smile.

He joined me in Hayama, and we did not marry, but developed a very comfortable partnership. We even worked out that we were very distant cousins. I had an antique seal in the form of an ivory orb that had belonged to someone on my father's family tree called Ball, and a book I had about coats of arms said it was also used by families with the name of Hall!

Ted and Derek and I had lots of fun and took many trips together. Ted was a great traveller and good at organizing tours. We spent many Christmases on the island of Saipan, and once circumnavigated the globe with Isabel Rendell taking in Australia and New Zealand as well as Tahiti, where we arrived in the middle of a celebration of its discoverer, Captain Wallis, Isabel's ancestor! She was received with exultation, for which I was able to be her interpreter.

I still miss Ted very much indeed. He had a splendid, subtle, truly British sense of humour, and best of all, he always had me 'on a pedestal'. I could do no wrong, which was so comforting. I remember being in a taxi with him and two Japanese men who were about to drop us off at the station after a Japan-British Society meeting. One of them said, 'Dorothy must have been a beauty when she was young', and Ted replied, 'She still is!' To hear him say that was like a draft of ambrosia although the Japanese were probably shocked, for they are brought up to refer to relatives disparagingly!

Ted enjoyed attending the annual Remembrance Day Services with Derek and me at the beautiful Commonwealth War Cemetery, where they had interred Boy's ashes that I brought back with me. The ravishing Princess Diana came there not long before her death, to lay a wreath at the grave of a soldier who had been a member of a regiment of which Her Highness was Patron. It was a hurriedly organized occasion, and the Ambassador had asked me to join them. I was surprised and highly honoured when the Princess paused by Boy's grave. Remembering Clifford Odet's lines, 'Do what is in your heart and you carry in yourself a revolution'. I *said* what was in my heart, and told her of my tremendous admiration of Her Royal Highness, and the way she had showered so much love and compassion on so many sufferers.

Ted liked Japan, except for one thing – 'the fandango' as he called it! The custom of having to take off one's shoes and leave them at the entrance. He loved Hayama, especially having lunch on the veranda. Ted's first words each morning were a question: 'Lunch on the veranda?' Boy loved it too. The first thing I had done after my mother died was to have a veranda constructed that overlooked the sea. It replaced two hydrangea bushes my mother did not want to remove.

Now, Derek and I spend as much time as we can on our veranda, communing with Nature and God, and so much Beauty: the shore, the elegant pine trees

– which I have always thought of as my brothers and sisters, since they were the same height as I was when they were planted. And the ocean. And that fabulous hill shape floating over the sea – my beloved Mount Fuji, majestic, glorious!

Dorothy Britton's Published Works

✦

MUSICAL COMPOSITIONS

Dover Beach for soprano and piano. Poem by Matthew Arnold. Prize Song 1943. Published by Mills College, California

Cantata: *And Certain Women Followed Him.* Schirmer, New York, 1955;1957

Suites: *Yedo Fantasy & Tokyo Impressions.* Capitol Records LP, 1957

20 Folksongs of Japan, new piano arrangements and English translation, circa 1958

Three Sea Hymns for *a cappella* chorus, in May Issue of Gassho Kai (Choral Club), Kawai Gakki Seisaku Sha, 1958

Windows of Joy and *Chapel Bell at Evening* for *a cappella* chorus. Poems by Yuki Hara. Published by Songs of England & America. Zen Ongaku Fu Shuppan Sha. 1961

Windows of Joy and *Chapel Bell at Evening* sung by Noriko Awaya, Toshiba Records. 1962

Series of British Folksongs for English Learners, arranged and sung by composer with Irish harp, Victor Records, 1965

Sacred solo, *Know Ye that the Lord He is God,* Boston Music Company, circa1967

Moku-moku mura no Ken-chan (Young Ken of Smokyville: First Steps in English)

Ken-chan no Boken. (Young Ken's Adventures: First Steps in English) Each story above illustrated by 48 manga paintings, with music by Dorothy Britton in 16 cassettes. Published by *Encyclopedia Brittanica* (Japan) Inc., circa 1968

Totto-chan, song in Britton's words and music, in 'Join the Fantastic World of Totto-chan' by Ikuo Koike, ALC. Inc. and Kodansha International, 1984

Chinoiserie: Histoire d'un Amour Oriental for mezzo soprano & string quartet, CD by Portland String Quartet with Rita Noel, Arabesque, New York. 1991.

BOOKS

In English:

National Parks of Japan (with Mary Sutherland), Kodansha International, Tokyo, 1980

The Japanese Crane, Bird of Happiness. KI, 1981. 4th printing 1986

Prince & Princess Chichibu: Two Lives Lived Above and Below the Clouds. Global Oriental, 2010

Japan Secondary School Bulletin. Volume 17 Number 6, School Publications Branch. Department of Education, Wellington, New Zealand

In Japanese:

ドロシーおばさんの上品な英会話 doroshii obasan no johin na eikaiwa (Aunt Dorothy's Good English Converstion) Jitsugyo no Nihon Sha, 1976

ワルツと囃子 warutsu to hayashi （In Waltz and Festival Rhythm) Essays; Jitsugyo no Nihon Sha, 1978

英会話おもしろセミナー eikaiwa omoshiro seminaa (English Conversation Fun Seminar) Bokuyo Sha, 1984
葉山日記 hayama nikki(Hayama Diary) in bi-monthly 'Japan Avenue'

TRANSLATIONS

Collected Songs of Ikuma Dan, Ongaku no Tomo Sha, 1958

Let's Sing in Japanese. Translations of Japanese songs, edited by Radio Japan. Illustrated by Kiyoshi Saito.Nippon Hoso Shuppan Kyokai (NHK Publishing Association), 1964

20 Folksongs of Japan. Translations and Britton's new piano arrangements. Illustrated by Kiyoshi Saito, 1965

Tu Tse-Chun by Ryunosuke Akutagawa, with woodcuts by Naoko Matsubara. Kodansha International, 1965

A Haiku Journey: Basho's Narrow Road to the Far North *and selected haiku.* Photographs by Dennis Stock. Translated and introduced by Dorothy Britton. Kodansha International,1974

Opera Yuzuru by Ikuma Dan, English translation by Dorothy G. Britton; German translation by E. Hartogs. Boosey & Hawkes, London, and Zen Ongaku-fu Shuppan Sha (Publishers of Complete Musical Scores), Tokyo,1976

(Also translated Ikuma Dan's operas Kikimimizukin (The Listening Cap) and *Yang Kwei-Fei.)*

A Haiku Journey: Basho's Narrow Road to a Far Province. Revised paperback edition without extra haiku, 1980. Many reprints and various editions.

Totto-chan, the Little Girl at the Window by Tetsuko Kuroyanagi. Kodansha International, 1982. Many reprints. Now published by Kodansha USA

Chihiro's Album of Words and Pictures by Chihiro Iwasaki. Kodansha International, 1989

The Girl with the White Flag. by Tomiko Higa. Kodansha International, 1991

'Voiceless Lament'' for soprano, baritone, narrator, chorus and orchestra. Poem by Kenji Miyazawa, music by Saburo Takata. Published by Ongaku-no-Tomo Sha, 1995

The Silver Drum. Memoir by Princess Chichibu, Global Oriental, 1996

The Spider's Thread & other stories, by Ryunosuke Akutagawa. Kodansha International, 1987, 7th printing 1996

Totto-Chan's Children: A Goodwill Journey to the Chidren of the World by Tetsuko Kuroyanagi, Kodansha International, 2000

ARTICLES IN MAGAZINES

Ilustrated articles in English specially commissioned by Asahi Shinbun's 18-volume annual *This is Japan*, 1954 - 1971:

Eels Broiled to Music (Japan's eel tradition)
Pig Boat to Paradise (Shikine Island)
Kanazawa: Water, Trees and Lordly Grace
Stony Beauty on the Island of Virtue (Shikoku's Tokushima Province)
Singing in the Snow (northern Honshu's folk music)

Regular illustrated series in Japanese entitled *hayama nikki* (Hayama Diary), in bi-monthly 'Japan Avenue', 1990 - 1994

Index

✦